Practical Remote Pair Programming

Best practices, tips, and techniques for collaborating productively with distributed development teams

Adrian Bolboacă

BIRMINGHAM—MUMBAI

Practical Remote Pair Programming

Group Product Manager: Aaron Lazar

Publishing Product Manager: Alok Dhuri

Senior Editor: Nitee Shetty

Content Development Editor: Tiksha Lad

Technical Editor: Rashmi Subhash Choudhari

Copy Editor: Safis Editing

Project Coordinator: Deeksha Thakkar

Proofreader: Safis Editing

Indexer: Vinayak Purushotham

Production Designer: Joshua Misquitta

First published: March 2021

Production reference: 1180321

Published by Packt Publishing Ltd.

Livery Place

35 Livery Street

Birmingham

B3 2PB, UK.

ISBN 978-1-80056-136-6

www.packt.com

To all the passionate software people out there: have fun coding!

– Adrian Bolboacă

Contributors

About the author

Adrian Bolboacă has international experience of more than 15 years in product and software development in small and large companies, having served customers from various European countries. He is an experienced trainer; he likes to teach passionate people from dynamic companies to exceed their potential by challenging their current activity model for better collaboration, performance, and satisfaction. Adrian has trained and coached individuals and teams on both the technical and organizational sides on topics such as architecture and software design, agile and lean transformations, visual management, continuous improvement, Scrum, Kanban, unit testing, TDD, pair-programming, clean code, rescuing legacy code, and much more.

I want to thank the Software Development Gang for their constant support and inspiration, especially Code Cop for making this book happen. Many thanks to my Mozaic Works colleagues who were patient while I was focusing on writing the book, and gave me the necessary slack. And, of course, many thanks to my many remote pair programming partners, of whom there are way too many to mention, and from whom I have learned all the aspects presented in this book.

About the reviewer

Steve Nield is a full-stack engineer and technical lead with 15 years' experience in building high-availability, low-latency web applications across a broad range of projects and company profiles. Steve started his career at Microsoft as an intern before becoming a contractor. Throughout his career, Steve has led large-scale product development and transformation projects with a proven track-record of introducing and driving the adoption of best practices through mentoring. He is currently focused on improving deployment practices through the introduction of CI/CD pipelines, test automation, and infrastructure as code; he believes that every engineer should be able to autonomously deploy safely and frequently to production.

Table of Contents

Preface

Section 1: Introduction to Pair Programming

1

Pair Programming and Its Necessity

The history of pair programming   4
Elucidating problems in pairs   5
Managing complexity   6

Sharpening our knowledge   7
Collaborative work   7
Leveling knowledge   8
Advancing knowledge   9

Gaining wisdom   10
Improving the system   11
Staff liquidity   11

Managing complexities in
complex domains   12
Managing complex domains   13
Difficult tasks   13
The fastest feedback code review   14

Minimizing the defect rate   14

Comfort for the future you   15
Code is more often read than written   15
Exploratory testing with pair
programming   16

Programming with your CEO   17
Social programming   18
The rubber duckling effect   19

How does pair programming
work?   20
Knowledge work and knowledge workers   20
Time well spent   20

Summary   21
Further reading   22

2

How Can Pair Programming Help?

Defining pair programming   24
Driver   24

Navigator   25
Trainer/facilitator   25

Boosting efficiency	26	**with other specializations**	39
Reducing task switching	27	Pairing with a tester	39
Taking breaks	28	Pairing with a UI designer	40
		Pairing with DevOps	40
Situations when pair		Pairing with a business analyst	41
programming can help	29	**Pair programming in practice**	41
Bettering efficiency	30	Learning new things or tricks	41
Improving technical skills	31	Being social – social programming	42
Aiding knowledge transfer	31		
Improving communication	33	**Pair programming cannot solve**	
Enhancing problem-solving capabilities	34	**everything**	43
Simplifying the existing code base	35	Unclear requirements	43
		Bad coding practices	43
Situations when pair		Tension within the team	43
programming is difficult	36	Tension within the organization	44
Working alone	37	Close to deployment time	44
Lack of safe space	37		
Only I want to pair from my team	38	**Summary**	44
		Further reading	45
Working better with colleagues			

3

Exploring Pair Programming Techniques and Styles

Understanding pair		Round-robin pairing	68
programming techniques	48	Promiscuous pairing	69
The Driver-Navigator technique	49	Selective pairing	70
The Pairing-Trainee technique	51		
The Beginner-Advanced technique	53	**How often do we need to pair?**	70
The Beginner-Beginner technique	55	Should you pair for the whole day?	71
The Ping-Pong technique	57	Should you pair daily?	71
		Should you pair weekly?	71
Improving pair programming			
with styles	59	**Exploring different**	
Unplanned pairing	59	**communication methods**	72
Traditional pairing	60	Aggressive communication	73
Elastic pairing	62	Submissive communication	73
Strong-style pairing	64	Assertive communication	73
		Making a difference with the right	
Organizing pair programming	68	words, tone, and clarity	74

Pair programming best practices 75

Taking notes while pair programming	76
Starting with some small talk	76
Emptying your cup	76
Debriefing	77
Dialogue courtesy	78
Building confidence – committing often and having good unit tests	79
Trusting your pair	79

Pair programming anti-patterns 80

Managing distractions	80
Centering the monitor	80
Dealing with the "I know it all" attitude	81
Addressing small pickings	81

Boosting productivity with remote pair programming 82

Summary 82

Further reading 83

Section 2: Remote Pair Programming

4

Using Pair Programming in a Distributed System

Technical requirements	**88**
Organizing remote pair programming	**88**
The purpose of remote pairing	89
Distributed team	93
Deciding on the scope	95
Duration	95
Pomodoro technique	96
Schedule	98
Kickoff	99
Concerns	102
Good practices of pairing	104
Anti-patterns	106

Performing regular retrospectives	**107**
How often we should retrospect	107
Retrospective techniques	108
What happens after a retrospective?	110
Improving the restrospectives continuously	**110**
Analyzing the results	110
Personal introspection	111
Tools analysis	111
Summary	**111**
Further reading	**112**

5

Remote Pair Programming Setup

Technical requirements	**114**
Checking the internet connection	**114**
Using a cable connection	115

Using a Wi-Fi connection	115
Using a portable router	115
Setting up video and audio	**116**
Setting up video	116

Checking the lighting   117
Choosing the camera   119
Understanding the camera's position   121
Checking the audio   121
Introducing audio   122
Choosing a microphone   122
Positioning your microphone   125
Use headphones, not loudspeakers   125
Mute pairing   126

Setting up the IDE   **127**
Key editor functionalities   128
Best IDEs for remote pair programming 128
Intellij IDEA   129
Best editor plugins for remote pair
programming   132

Setting up screen sharing   **134**
Introducing TeamViewer   134

Introducing AnyDesk   135
Introducing Screen   136
Introducing Use Together   137
Introducing Tuple   137
Introducing Zoom   138
Introducing Google Meet   139
Introducing Skype   140

Learning to use source control   **141**
Source control tools   141
Commit often   143
Ensemble commits   143
Rotation   144

**Using two computers for coding
and
remote screening**   **145**
Summary   **145**
Further reading   **146**

6
Remote Pair Programming-Specific Techniques and Styles

**Recap of main concepts of pair
programming**   **148**
Understanding general setup   **149**
**Understanding the remote
driver-navigator technique**   **150**
Remote setup   150
Remote specifics – driver   151
Remote specifics – navigator   152

Remote ping-pong technique   **154**
Remote setup   155
Remote specifics – driver   155
Remote specifics – navigator   156

**Remote beginner-advanced
technique**   **156**
Remote setup   157

Remote specifics – driver   157
Remote specifics – navigator   158

Traditional pairing style   **159**
Remote setup   159
Remote specifics   159

**Remote elastic pair
programming style**   **161**
Remote setup   162
Remote specifics   162

Remote strong style   **163**
Remote setup   165
Remote specifics   165

Good remote practices   **168**
Remote breaks   168

Secondary communication channel 168   Summary   170
Remote commit approach   169

Section 3: Tools to Enhance Remote Pair Programming

7

Video and Audio

Recap of what we have learned   Speaking into the microphone   179
so far   174   Using an audio compressor   180
General technical aspects   174   Performing soundcheck   182
Audio is more important than video 174 Monitoring the sound   183
Video settings   175   Adding a pop filter   184
Screen sharing settings   175
Quality sound and video for the win 175 Enhancing speech   184
                                        Employing diction   185
Learning how to enhance video 176   Choosing words   185
Looking into the camera   176   Warming up your voice   185
Using a green screen   177
Using a virtual background   178   Summary   186

Learning to enhance audio   179

8

Source Control Rules

Recap of the source control   Committing before taking a break, in a
rules   188   stable state   194
Using source control   188   Committing when the preparatory
                                        refactoring is done   195
Improving source control usage 189   Committing when one characterization
Using the commit types   190   test is done   195
Understanding commit   Committing when one unit test is green 196
heuristics   193   Summary   198
Committing when part of a feature is   Further reading   199
done   194
Committing when all the tests are
written, and green, for a user scenario 194

9

Remote Access

Recapping the rules of remote pairing	202	Relying on tools	206
Understanding how remote access tools work	202	Bug magnet	206
		Security for remote access	207
TeamViewer	203	Summary	209
AnyDesk	204	Further reading	210
Screen	204	Why subscribe?	211
Chrome Remote Desktop	205		

Other Books You May Enjoy

Index

Preface

When I started programming, I had no idea how important teamwork is, as I only learned about programming languages, mathematics, and tools during my studies. It didn't take me long to understand that you need to learn from your colleagues in order to make the profession of programming a nice experience. After a while, I started learning about more and more things, and mentorship began to help me a lot. Having someone, or multiple people, from whom to learn intensively really boosted my career, and I think I burned some steps faster than others, just because of mentorship.

Pair programming was one of the activities I was doing with my mentors, either face to face, or remotely, even in times gone by when the internet wasn't that good. I started intensively using pair programming during the Coderetreat events I was facilitating, a full-day learning experience organized by volunteers for passionate coders. Since I was traveling all over Europe with Coderetreat for a good few years, I started to get to know people all over the place, and I wanted to learn more from them. So remote pair programming was the natural approach.

Remote pair programming is now my main learning tool, besides reading articles and books, and having discussions with people who are smarter than me. Working together, trying, and struggling together on a problem is challenging but also fun and rewarding. I hope that after you have read this book, you will find that remote pair programming can and should be challenging but also fun and rewarding.

Who this book is for

This book is mainly for programmers, at any seniority or skill level, but as I have learned from pairing with many people, anyone can learn how to work together as a team better. So, I highly encourage anyone who works in IT to give it a try and learn from it how to pair, learn, improve and have fun while pairing.

What this book covers

Chapter 1, Pair Programming and Its Necessity, helps you find out why we need pair programming and how it can be used.

Chapter 2, How Can Pair Programming Help?, helps you master how to boost learning and create a pleasant environment for your team with pair programming.

Chapter 3, Usual Pair Programming Techniques and Styles, checks what the appropriate collaboration technique and style for your team is by using pair programming.

Chapter 4, Using Pair Programming in a Distributed System, helps you learn how to boost your distributed team's productivity by using pair programming.

Chapter 5, Remote Pair Programming Setup, covers getting the gear and setting things up for real professional remote pair programming.

Chapter 6, Remote Pair Programming Specific Techniques and Styles, checks how you can adapt your remote work with specific techniques and styles, adapted for remote pair programming.

Chapter 7, Voice and Audio, discusses how when we work remotely, voice and audio are very important, and you will learn how to use them like a pro in this chapter.

Chapter 8, Source Control, covers using source control as part of a programmer's job, and you will learn some general good practices and some tweaks for remote pair programming in this chapter.

Chapter 9, Remote Access, looks at how we cannot have remote pair programming without remote access, and you will learn how to use it well and safely here.

To get the most out of this book

You don't need much setup in the beginning. You only need your regular computer, with your regular coding environment. During the book, you will gradually see how you can improve your setup for remote pair programming.

Download the color images

We also provide a PDF file that has color images of the screenshots/diagrams used in this book. You can download it here: `https://static.packt-cdn.com/downloads/9781800561366_ColorImages.pdf`.

Conventions used

There are a number of text conventions used throughout this book.

`Code in text`: Indicates code words in text, database table names, folder names, filenames, file extensions, pathnames, dummy URLs, user input, and Twitter handles. Here is an example: "Mount the downloaded `WebStorm-10*.dmg` disk image file as another disk in your system."

A block of code is set as follows:

```
commit d6a3b90e95b5e4f356c4236b55707a21465ca67n
Author: Adrian Bolboacă <adi@email.email>
Date:    Thu May 28 09:05:15 2020 +0200
```

When we wish to draw your attention to a particular part of a code block, the relevant lines or items are set in bold:

```
commit d6a3b90e95b5e4f356c4236b55707a21465ca67t
Author: Adrian Bolboacă adi@email.email>
Date:    Thu May 28 09:05:15 2020 +0200

     Solved defect: AB99238. The correct name of the start
```

> **Tips or important notes**
> Appear like this.

Get in touch

Feedback from our readers is always welcome.

General feedback: If you have questions about any aspect of this book, mention the book title in the subject of your message and email us at `customercare@packtpub.com`.

Errata: Although we have taken every care to ensure the accuracy of our content, mistakes do happen. If you have found a mistake in this book, we would be grateful if you would report this to us. Please visit `www.packtpub.com/support/errata`, selecting your book, clicking on the Errata Submission Form link, and entering the details.

Piracy: If you come across any illegal copies of our works in any form on the Internet, we would be grateful if you would provide us with the location address or website name. Please contact us at copyright@packt.com with a link to the material.

If you are interested in becoming an author: If there is a topic that you have expertise in and you are interested in either writing or contributing to a book, please visit authors.packtpub.com.

Reviews

Please leave a review. Once you have read and used this book, why not leave a review on the site that you purchased it from? Potential readers can then see and use your unbiased opinion to make purchase decisions, we at Packt can understand what you think about our products, and our authors can see your feedback on their book. Thank you!

For more information about Packt, please visit packt.com.

Section 1: Introduction to Pair Programming

This section is a first touch on the topic of pair programming, where we get to understand the topic, when to apply pair programming, and how to start.

This section has the following chapters:

- *Chapter 1, Pair Programming and Its Necessity*
- *Chapter 2, How Can Pair Programming Help?*
- *Chapter 3, Usual Pair Programming Techniques and Styles*

1
Pair Programming and Its Necessity

Pair programming can be easy to use when you are focusing on building software that is of high quality. You, as a programmer, can pair with other programmers to find quicker solutions to your problems and get better results. Furthermore, you can pair with other colleagues: testers, analysts, (dev)ops, security, and so on.

Pair programming in itself is simple: you have a *driver* who writes the code and a *navigator* who oversees the code. The two are roles that can change slower or faster, depending on your context. We will learn about them in more detail as this book progresses.

You can use pair programming in many moments. Typically, we pair program naturally when we are stuck and ask for a colleague's help. Also, we can schedule pairing sessions as a regular activity. Some like to pair daily, or just a few times per week. It's a matter of context and where it helps you get better results.

Usually, you pair program in the office, at your desk, or at your colleague's desk. You can take your laptop(s) and pair in a meeting room on a big screen, or on a terrace when the weather's nice. Or, you can remote pair program by using specific tools to pair with people wherever in the world, as long as they have good internet.

Continuous learning, improved quality, fewer defects, managing complex problems, and solving specific problems faster are just a few reasons to use pair programming. Because programmers deal with a mass of knowledge, wrapping your head around all the essential details with another colleague helps your endeavor with speed and quality.

In this chapter, we will cover the following topics:

- The history of pair programming
- Elucidating problems in pairs
- Sharpening knowledge with collaboration
- Gaining wisdom
- Managing complexities in complex domains
- Comfort for the future you
- Programming with your CEO
- How does pair programming work?

The history of pair programming

Pair programming has been around for a long time in the history of software development, even from the early days, when programming meant plugging in some wires into a control dashboard or inserting punch cards into a reader in order to compile your program.

It's just that people who used to program back in the day didn't call it pair programming; they called it simple, plain *programming*. You needed to do things in pairs because of the wires or the cards that were cumbersome to use.

Then came the era of industrial programming where, little by little, pushed by the need for automatization and computers being more affordable, programmers were working more and more alone. It was an age of simpler programs, but it took a long time to write, compile, check, fix, improve, write, compile, and so on.

After a while, computers started becoming more powerful and even more affordable. So, companies started automating more complex parts of their business flows. We are talking about financial systems, travel, trade, and so on. You had a complex domain already, but programmers were working alone, as in any other factory. They had a boss, like in any other factory, and a manager, like in any other factory.

The only problem with comparing factory workers with programmers is that programmers need to solve problems that are from non-routine work, while factory workers had a clear routine that might have been subject to change every once in a while. That is the moment when the concept of the *knowledge worker* appeared in the management literature:

"Every knowledge worker in a modern organization is an "executive" if, by virtue of his position or knowledge, he is responsible for a contribution that materially affects the capacity of the organization to perform and to obtain results."

- Peter Drucker in The Effective Executive (1966)

Pair programming then reappeared in some areas, and younger programmers read about the older ways of programming. They started using it with great success, and it felt very natural to have two people coding for a task. Plain pair programming is a simple system of managing complexity and gaining better results.

Elucidating problems in pairs

The best way of explaining why pair programming works is that two people can understand how to write some code better than just one programmer. It is true that when we code trivial parts of the system, pair programming is unnecessary – even counterproductive. So, it's important to choose when to *pair program* and when to *solo program*.

Here are a few situations where pair programming works great, and where the **two heads are better than one** rule applies:

- A junior programmer learning from a senior programmer.
- A new programmer in a team learns from an existing programmer in the team.
- Fresh tasks are assigned to the team, and two people can tackle the problem better and faster.
- A programmer learns new practice (that is, test-driven development, unit testing, and so on).

As a rule of thumb, it is a good idea to use pair programming when we have a task with higher complexity, either the technical or the business side. It's good to acknowledge that programmers are more likely to make mistakes in complex or unknown areas of code.

There are situations where we'll have simple, trivial tasks that don't necessarily need pairing, or even more, where pairing would be just a waste of time for at least one of the two. Often, it's a good idea to have this discussion with the whole team. After all, it should be the decision for the whole team on how they use their common time, what the learning or improvement focus is in the next period, and where they can't afford pairing because they need to deliver faster.

Should I pair? Before you start a new task, ask yourself the following questions:

- How would I benefit from using pair programming?
- How would the team/product benefit from using pair programming?
- Would we learn anything useful for the team by pairing?
- Would pair programming delay a delivery?
- Would pairing on this task be boring or superfluous?

These questions could help you and your team decide if it's worth investing in pair programming for that specific task. Yes, it is an investment, and you should treat every decision with objectivity and respect for the rest of the team. After all, two heads are better than one in some situations, though in other situations, where even one head wouldn't be used too much, using pair programming would just be a waste of time and energy.

Managing complexity

Following the idea that two heads are better than one, we can use pair programming to manage better complexity.

Let's face it: programmers almost never do the exact same task. It might be that the domain is similar, or identical, but there are so many moving parts in the whole ecosystem, such as programming language, frameworks, external or internal use libraries, programming patterns, architecture patterns, business domain variations, performance, security, scalability, and so on. A programmer needs to think about all these and more when writing code. That is why we can make a strong case when we say complexity is inherent in most programming tasks.

Having two people who look at all the aspects of the code is clearly beneficial. There is a *driver* who writes the code and a *navigator* who oversees the code, thinks about possible next steps, thinks about possible caveats, and improves the code while it is being written.

Humans only have one brain, and we can only focus our full attention on one thing. We can pivot our focus from one aspect to another, but that is tiring and during the switch, we might lose some details. That is why the driver focuses on writing the code while looking at low-level details such as code syntax, code logic, framework/library usage, or code formatting. And, at the same time, the navigator focuses on high-level details such as design aspects, architecture concerns, performance, security, and so on.

After all, what pair programming does is split the overall complexity into smaller, less complex parts that are easier to manage. These smaller parts are managed by two people, who use the clear responsibilities that are attributed to the driver and the navigator.

A good guideline is necessary for clarifying the driver and navigator roles before starting the pair programming session. Even if we have paired many times before, or if we are at the beginning of our first pair programming session, it's a good idea to clarify what each of the two pairs will do so that we can manage complexity better. We need to take into account the experience, knowledge, and skill level of both programmers before we start.

In this section, we discussed the history of pair programming and how pair programming can help you. It's a good option to solve complex problems we consider difficult and troublesome to solve on our own. You have now a few good guidelines about when to use pair programming or when it's better to solo program. Next, we'll discuss the various ways we can pair program, depending on our teams.

Sharpening our knowledge

There are several contexts that need to be accounted for when you're using pair programming for learning; that is, collaboration, alignment, and improvement. Let's learn how to pair program in a different way, depending on the team's current level and knowledge uniformity.

Collaborative work

The idea of collective code ownership existed in programmers' lives even before the existence of pair programming. This means that all the code that we write as individuals is our code, and anyone can change it as per their needs. We don't have codebase areas that are owned by their authors. We don't need the author's permission to change anything. However, we do need to obey some rules that can be summed into two areas: *improve the code* and *don't introduce defects*.

Pair programming cannot work without you having collective code ownership. There are two immediate effects that occur when you're implementing collective code ownership: it's difficult to know the other author's code, and you remove some bottlenecks as there is no need to wait for someone to do their task.

The most effective way to know a particular author's code is to program with the author. Due to this, pair-programming opens the door to spreading knowledge within the team. There are multiple ways of spreading knowledge in the team, depending on our focus in the short-, medium-, and long-term future. We can focus on people and then decide if we want to improve their skills. Similarly, we can focus on the product/system and then decide if we want to improve the team's knowledge about it. In fact, we should do both, but take the timing into account. Maybe there are moments when it's more appropriate to learn new skills, as we may have good knowledge about the system, or vice versa. If a completely new feature arrives, with its own different and difficult domain logic, it's obvious that we should focus on that, and it's not a good moment to learn new skills.

After all, a team should be more than the sum of its parts; that's when you will see collaborative work. Any team member should be able to help another, and any team member should be open to new skills, practices, tools, and system or domain knowledge, as long as it evolves the overall delivery capacity.

Collaborative work means that we understand and act under the underlying principle that the team needs to work well together, to have continuous improvement. Pair programming is a manifestation of collaborative work, a tool of fair collaboration that fosters productivity and enjoyment for good quality products.

Leveling knowledge

A team needs to have the same minimal level of knowledge on essential topics, be it related to business as well as technical. What better way to level knowledge than two people who have different levels of knowledge to work together?

Of course, this whole process is not necessarily easy, especially if you were used to working alone. It might feel intrusive, cumbersome, frustrating, or even annoying. That is why I wouldn't recommend anyone starting to level knowledge with pair programming without some sort of management or outside coaching.

Using pair programming to level knowledge is a great approach, which comes with a few short-term disadvantages, along with a few long-term ones. First, in the short term, you will see the team being more tired, often with more stress and them delivering below par. Nevertheless, during the next few pair programming sessions, you will feel less and less tired and you will get used to this way of working. In the long term, we have the benefits of real collective code ownership, where anyone can change the code in any part of the system, without the fear of introducing defects.

When we start to level the knowledge, we need to explain the process really well to the team; that is, we need to explain why we are doing this, how it will be done, how long we expect it to last, and what the possible short-term and long-term effects may be. After that, a good practice is to start collecting some tasks that are appropriate for pair programming with the purpose to level knowledge. We don't aim to do full-time pair programming, because it will be extremely difficult for everyone to cope. Rather, in the beginning, it is preferable to do 1-2 hours per day of pair programing. A good practice is to have the first few days be completed under the supervision of a technical coach, with all the pairs in a room and the coach observing and giving advice on how to pair program in an effective way. After that, the technical coach can remain as an adviser, as many questions remain on how to effectively work as a pair.

Advancing knowledge

Once the team has a similar minimal level of knowledge about the business and technical side, the next step is to think about improvements. Often, while leveling knowledge through pair programming, every team member starts having ideas about how things could go better. So, don't miss the opportunity and note down every idea that appears. Often, taking notes about what you would like to learn next is a good approach so that when the time comes to pair program with the focus on advancing knowledge, you have a clear idea of what to do next.

During sessions of advancing knowledge, you can involve a technical coach as well, to make sure that the focus remains on that specific learning activity. A technical coach would make sure there is a prioritized learning backlog for each of the team members, and that they have the time and space to learn.

Let's take an example of a programmer who knows Java and would like to learn JavaScript to help their team's endeavor to implement their next feature, which is user interface-intensive. For that, an experienced JavaScript programmer would pair with a Java programmer. They would take an appropriate task that was in line for JavaScript and work on it together. Of course, the time to finish that task will be significantly higher when the two programmers work together in the beginning, because learning is involved. But after 2-3 weeks of daily pair programming sessions, usually, the time taken to complete such a task is reduced. Now, the Java programmer can take on easy JavaScript tasks on their own, helping the team deliver faster.

Using pair programming to advance knowledge is a very good practice to help the team solve long-waiting lines at specific specialties. In our example, what would have happened if all the Java programmers had to wait their turn until the only JavaScript programmer reached their request from the long list of tasks they needed to perform? We want to avoid that as much as possible. And the solution is not to give all the difficult tasks at the back to the most experienced programmer – we should do the opposite if we want to improve our productivity in the long term. We want to spread the knowledge that is needed in the near future inside the team. In practice, this means that the most experienced people would teach volunteers how to perform simple tasks, thus relieving them of the trivial tasks and letting them focus on the intricate ones. This attitude can bring a huge difference to the overall timeline and success of your software product.

The idea of improving your knowledge through practice is very old. It comes from the medieval times of manual crafts. We can learn from those times and take what can be applied today. Learning while working with someone is very powerful as it brings more positive aspects to the table: observing, working with expert supervision, discussing aspects of the craft, and thus understanding how to do the work better. Now, we will move on and discuss how we can improve our current knowledge base when we pair program.

Gaining wisdom

We can learn and get wiser as we gain knowledge of the profession. Getting wiser can happen by itself, with active learning, constant work, and passion. We can also boost learning and, by doing so, get to the goal of being wiser faster. And the wiser we are, the more we see that we understood less than we initially thought. So, we need to learn some more. Learning never stops. In this section, we will understand this in the context of pair programming.

Improving the system

We can also use pair programming sessions to improve parts of the system. It's a similar approach to advancing our knowledge, but in this case, we are talking about specific parts of the system.

Especially in complex systems, there are people who know it very well; that is, specialists in the domain, logic, and particularities of that part of the system. Usually, if you are a specialist, everyone comes to you to ask questions. But you may also have other things to do – other tasks or parts of the system that you need to take care of. That is when you become a bottleneck for the whole system. The team, coach, manager, or anyone else will need to observe this situation and come up with a plan to pass their knowledge to a few other people. A good practice is to have at least three very knowledgeable people on a specific part of the system. This helps if you want to optimize your development for a fast flow, fast feedback type of development.

When it comes to passing knowledge to a part of the system, we can talk about programmers, testers, analysts, ops, security, or any other role in the team. So, pair programming can be a tool to make pairs such as programmer-analyst, programmer-tester, and so on. We can also extend the whole pair programming approach and lose the programming part. We could have two analysts, for example, pair up in the same way: expert-beginner. But if we are talking about experts and beginners on that particular part of the system, their overall experience wouldn't need to be that important.

Once we've removed these knowledge bottlenecks, we can start thinking about improving the system. Pair programming, or plain pairing, will help the team deliver faster, with some initial time well-invested for the long-term future of our product.

Staff liquidity

This practical approach to advance knowledge, where the most knowledgeable individual would teach others who are less knowledgeable, rather than performing the most difficult tasks, has a name: **staff liquidity**. The concept of staff liquidity was introduced by Chris Matts during an article back in 2013 (a link for this has been provided in the *Further reading* section).

Chris Matts explains that there are four levels of knowledge anyone can have for a particular skill or part of the system:

- *0 – "I know nothing!"*
- *1 – "I can run it."*
- *2 – "I can tweak it or bug fix it."*
- *3 – "I can redesign or refactor it." / "I OWN it!"*

Here are the steps we follow to implement this in our organization:

1. We need to make a list of skills we need to have (for example, Java, JavaScript, unit testing, continuous integration, and so on) and a list of system parts that we need to know (for example, frontend, backend, database, and so on).

2. We must then list the names of all the team members, one after another. We use the *0-3* marking system to mark the current situation, in a matrix form.

3. Finally, we need to make sure we have at least three people at level *3* for each line in the matrix. *How do we get there?* Via learning sessions with pair programming. Budget the time needed for learning and get pairing!

Of course, staff liquidity goes beyond pair programming, but we will only focus on how suited it is for boosting pair programming's extensive usage. You can use staff liquidity in any aspect of the organization where you need to improve a team member's skills, alleviate bottlenecks, increase time to market, or accelerate feedback cycles.

In this section, we looked at some ways to get wiser, and we looked at systemic thinking for advancing learning. Staff liquidity is a very powerful concept that needs to be in every senior professional's toolkit. We can be so much more efficient, and deliver so much more quality, just by organizing ourselves better. And as a bonus, our environment's spirits and morale increases a lot. Next, we'll study how we can conquer complexities in our development systems.

Managing complexities in complex domains

One of the main reasons software development is difficult is because we deal with complexity. Let's see how we can use pair programming in complex, difficult situations, when it helps us, and when we should use other tools instead.

Managing complex domains

The more complex the business domain, the more you need pair programming. And let's face it: even the simplest business domain is complex nowadays.

In areas such as banking, trade, or travel, you can expect from the start that you will have a lot of complexity on your hands. Typically, code written in complex areas tends to be worse in the beginning. It's the "first half-baked draft" that writers so often refer to. This is because writing code is not that different from writing an article, a novel, or a series of novels if you work in a very large organization.

Writers say that it's a good idea to quickly write what's on your mind. No matter how much you struggle to write the perfect first version of your text, there is only one conclusion: it will be horrible. The first draft should be like a lump of clay that you shape after several iterations of reading and improvement. The only problem is that we have a blind spot for errors we've created ourselves. That is why, especially in a complex domain, code review is always a good idea. Or even better, we can speed up the code review with pair programming.

Iterative development happens even in the smallest of programming tasks. We create the simplest form of solution, and then we ask for feedback. The beauty of pair programming is that this feedback comes almost instantly from our pair. Because of this, we feel that we can tackle complex problems easier if we work in a pair.

Difficult tasks

Sometimes, we might feel overwhelmed by looking at a complex task. And we might even procrastinate, just fearing that the task is too difficult, or thinking that we need to prepare more in order to face the new task. This usually happens with tasks that are in a new area for us, something that just attacks our self-perceived competencies. Working in a pair will reduce that fear. It's not just me who's fighting the dragon; I have a pair and if something bad happens, we can think about what to do together. Often, that thought makes me feel like we can get through it.

Pair programming on difficult tasks needs to be done between programmers who have the same level of experience. It doesn't make any sense to have a senior-junior pair, as the junior will be completely lost. The only good solution is to have a senior-senior pair, with the focus on getting things done, rather than a learning focus.

There is this misconception that all pair programming sessions are about learning. In fact, especially in complex domains, we have many more pair programming sessions focused on solving tasks and getting things done.

Context is important. If you have more time at hand, it's a good practice to do pair programming both with highly experienced programmers to advance the task, and with less experienced programmers with the purpose of them learning what the most experienced pair is doing. But if we don't have the time at hand and we need to deliver, we should focus on getting things done. Then, after the delivery or deployment, we need to plan some learning sessions for the less experienced programmers.

The fastest feedback code review

A good coding practice is **code review**. It has been around since the beginning of programming as a format for formally inspecting code. It can be used to improve the code's format and logic, or as a way to distribute coding or domain knowledge. Typically, the code is written and then there are one or more programmers who will formally review the code. The programmer who wrote the code reads the reviewer's comments and improves the code. Then, the code is passed through the code review once more. This keeps happening until the reviewers accept the code as it is. Because the subsequent code reviews can take a long time, the code can only be said to be *done* after many days. It can even take a few weeks for the initial code to pass the cycle of reviews and changes.

Let's think about how the code review can be done while the code is written. We have a driver, the person who writes the code, and the navigator, the person who observes mistakes, incorrect names, logical errors, domain mistakes, performance issues, and so on.

If we go by the classical code review format, we have a few weeks to get from the initial form to the final form, but with pair programming, you only have a few hours. Also, by using pair programming, we remove the overhead of writing improvements, reading improvements, and having meetings to understand the given feedback. Also, the overhead of learning how to use a tool for code review disappears.

Since it is a good practice to have more points of view when we're doing code reviews, we could do the same with pair programming. We can change the pairs often, so that more programmers can look over the same code while working on the feature.

Minimizing the defect rate

One direct outcome you would expect is to have less defects in the code that was written by using pair programming. The reason for this is simple: *two heads are better than one*.

The cost of fixing a defect becomes higher and higher as time passes. The classical approach of fixing bugs, analysis - coding - testing - analysis - coding - ... - done, can take a long time for a new feature. And the defects that were not caught in this very long cycle will be even more difficult to catch later, after the code is in production. The more time passes by, the more difficult it will be for anyone involved in that task to remember what is going on. That is why we need to find ways to minimize the defect rate right from the beginning. We can maximize the feedback loops in order to minimize the defect rate.

Besides having a cross-functional team that uses practices such as continuous integration, unit testing, or test-driven development, a very good practice that's used to minimize defects is pair programming. With pair programming, you can catch simple logical mistakes in a second, just because you have a navigator who is always watching and trying to understand the code the driver writes. You cannot have a shorter feedback loop than a few seconds when you're fixing a defect!

Complexity is a hard thing to grasp, especially when you are in the middle of the action. It's like wanting to count how many trees are in a forest, while you are in the forest. The first thing you must do is go back a few steps and get a bigger picture of everything. Apparently, obvious things can help us: fast feedback, transparency, openness, and close collaboration.

Next, we'll discuss how we can make our future selves' lives more comfortable!

Comfort for the future you

I am always stupid in my own eyes when I look at the code that I wrote 6 months ago. I do get it, but I would have liked to have written it better, in a more elegant fashion. I always have mixed feelings: I feel good because it means I learned a lot in the meantime, but I also feel like I haven't done a good enough job. This is a problem for any content creator, writer, programmer, and so on. Let's learn how to create comfort for our future selves by putting quality first.

Code is more often read than written

We often look at some of our older code and reading it is difficult. We know that we work in a complex domain, where we need to know so many things just to get started. We need to know the technology, the syntax, the business domain jargon, and so on. Considering that we know all that, it still so happens that older code (even from a few months back) is very difficult to understand.

The question is: *why did we write such a bad code?* It has happened to me more than once when I have had to look at some older code, got annoyed, and said this code is a mess. Then, when I looked at the author, it was none other than me. This illustrates that I'm maybe a better programmer now than I used to be. Or, it says that I needed more improvement feedback on that code, either via a code review or a strict pair while writing it.

If, during our pair programming sessions, we focus on the readability, clarity, and usability of the code at hand, we will certainly have better results in the long term. It's often not enough for just one person to write the code and ship it. There are always improvements that we can make to that initial code.

Think about all the people who read your code, and how much time and effort would be spared if we took the time to write some code that is easy to understand. Of course, this comes with a cost, but we need to balance the time it takes to write the code and the time we imagine will be spent reading and understanding the code.

Pair programming comes with some help for this situation. One of the navigator's main jobs is to read the code over and over again, from top to bottom, and think about how easy it would be to understand it. Then, they need to stop the driver and come up with improvement ideas on naming, domain jargon, coherence, brevity, and so on.

Exploratory testing with pair programming

Imagine that you have a programming task and a tester sits next to you, immediately testing the code you have written. Well, that might be an exaggeration, but at least the tester is doing a live code review with a clear focus on testing.

The tester's mindset is to think about how the system under test would be destroyed, while the programmer's mindset is to think about how the system needs to be created. Without a doubt, a programmer is highly optimistic and believes all will be good. A tester is highly pessimistic and sees potential cracks in the system, including errors, issues, and so on. This *optimist + pessimist* couple is great because together, they can spot the correct implementations, errors, defects, or bad names from the code.

Exploratory testing is a way of testing where test cases are not created in advance and repeated, but rather the testers check the system on the fly. The tester looks at the product or explores it, with the fresh eye of a new user that will not respect the direct, clear path of using the system. A tester would try to fill in wrong data, or almost wrong data, go back and forth through the user flows, they might refresh or write really fast in some areas, or click on a button frequently, all to see what might happen and to explore if the system was taught to be resilient enough in such circumstances. Exploratory testing requires a different mindset, and it involved a lot more than what I've just stated. But there is a clear difference between checking a system based on a set of plans and checking a system by using exploratory testing.

When talking to testers who are experienced with doing exploratory testing, I have often heard that code review is a form of exploratory testing, but on the code. Furthermore, on-the-fly code review is an improved form of exploratory testing. Testers might call this format of pair programming (*programmer driving + tester navigating*) exploratory testing as well. It's revealing that this is the form of exploratory testing that has the fastest feedback loop of seconds or minutes.

Using exploratory testing techniques on the fly, while the programmer is writing the code, is the fastest way of minimizing the number of defects that occur when a tester is involved.

Next, we'll explore how to interact with peers who are not specifically from or understand the workings of a technical world.

Programming with your CEO

Business is why we build software. If it weren't for ideas that bring value to other people, then software wouldn't exist. Programming has a lot of jargon, a language not accessible to non-specialists, that is not easily understood by all. But if we were to work with non-specialists, they should understand what we are doing as well, as long as they know the business. So, in this section, we are going to discuss some aspects of improving our interactions with our peers.

Social programming

We may want to improve the social interactions inside the team, and pair programming is a good practice for that. While working on our computers, we must remember that we work for and with other human beings. Quite often, and unfortunately not always, the code we write will be used in a direct or indirect form by many people. So, it's important to also remember the social aspect of programming.

At the same time, our team, our product team, and our organization are made up of people who can learn and teach many interesting things. Because of this, we can take advantage of this and use pair programming as a way to learn faster from our peers.

Social programming means that we want to learn, share, and work with other people, explaining what we know while being humble and learning from others with openness and curiosity. Pair programming enables all these, as we can take the opportunity to learn and share. This mindset is extremely beneficial for all the team members, as it fosters continuous overall advancement in all areas.

Pair programming is a tool that's very appropriate for social programming, as you're trying to improve the social interactions of a team. Often, people think about pair programming as a tool to code together, to minimize defects, and that's it. But almost half of the activities I do as a technical coach with teams have to do with soft skills, social skills, or human interactions.

It's important to know how to talk to your colleagues, give and receive feedback, and communicate with other roles or managers from the rest of the organization. I always ask programmers: *how would you explain this code if you were to pair program with your CEO?* This situation might sound funny or absurd, but if you can clearly explain to a CEO, without the whole technical jargon, what that code is doing, it means that you know what you are doing really well. And it also means that you have excellent communication skills.

As a side note, during a community event that I was facilitating, while the programmers were pairing, a CEO appeared. He heard about this event and he was curious what was going on. Nobody had any idea about his role, and he joined, paired, and discussed just like any other attendee. Only after the event did I find out that he wasn't really a programmer. Imagine if you behaved the same if you knew that your CEO was joining you during a pair programming session. This is a good example of social programming, even without programmers being involved.

The rubber duckling effect

One particularly interesting way of using our cognitive structure is by utilizing the **rubber duckling** effect, or **teddy bear** pair programming. A debugging study that was performed with students in 2012 showed that when we have a problem, the best solution is to verbalize it. When explaining our problem in detail, our brain works in such a way that we start finding the solution for the problem at hand ourselves. Apparently, we don't need to talk with someone to give us advice; rather, we just need to talk, even alone, and in most situations, we'll find the solution ourselves:

> ". . . [an] effective technique is to explain your code to someone else. This will often cause you to explain the bug to yourself. Sometimes it takes no more than a few sentences, followed by an embarrassed "Never mind; I see what's wrong. Sorry to bother you." This works remarkably well; you can even use non-programmers as listeners. One university computer center kept a teddy bear near the help desk. Students with mysterious bugs were required to explain them to the teddy bear before they could speak to a human counsellor."
>
> – Kernighan, B. W. and R. Pike (1999). The Practice of Programming. Reading, Massachusetts, Addison-Wesley

Pair programming takes advantage of this quirk. A good practice is, even before we start coding, to explain to our partner what we want to do. If there are gray areas where we don't have an answer, we will find an answer just while talking. And for the majority of the areas where we really don't have an answer, our partner will help us. Typically, during a pair programming session, we either solve all the problems in the beginning, or while they appear, or we have a blockage and we need to talk to our colleagues. The first situation occurs far more often, but there are situations where we'll need to have a break or have a discussion with other colleagues.

Of course, we can use the rubber duckling effect even without having a person in front of us. I personally use a teddy bear and I explain what bothers me. I know that it may sound weird, but you need to try it for yourself without a lot of judgment. You will see how much it helps.

Yes, it sounds silly to talk to a rubber duck, a teddy bear, or your favorite toy animal, but it works. And hey, reach out for your inner child and think about playing a bit. Being playful is a lot more useful for our imagination than being serious. Often, good solutions come when you start playing and open the imagination door.

Next, we will learn how to use pair programming within our respective jobs.

How does pair programming work?

We want to be responsible for our own successes and failures. That is why we need to take some decisions into our own hands. When we really know some things can be better, or how a thing will be better, we need to fight for it. Sometimes, we win, sometimes, we lose, but it's important to have an intellectual debate about how to use our time, what we should learn, and the options for the tools and technologies appropriate for the job.

Knowledge work and knowledge workers

Programmers deal with knowledge every day. They take some raw information, and they try to shape it into systems. This whole effort is not a simple one; it requires a lot of analysis power, abstract thinking, and discipline. It is always an endeavor of partial results, slow progress, frustration, and enjoyment.

Continuing this train of thought and using the concept of knowledge workers that we introduced previously, we can conclude that programmers are knowledge workers. And not only programmers, but everyone in any software development team is a knowledge worker. This view is essential when it comes to thinking about the activities that we need to perform in a software development team.

Learning is not optional when we're dealing with knowledge work. I often get this question: *how can I convince my manager to let us learn X?* If a software development team doesn't learn, they are doomed to create low-quality products, with high maintenance costs. Looking just at the momentary time costs of learning is a very narrow and unjust way of looking at this. We always need to look at both the short- and long-term benefits of whatever activity we set out to complete.

Use pair programming as a tool so that you become a *knowledgeable knowledge worker*, with the appetite to learn more, always improve, and strive for the best. Have pair programming sessions where you focus on optimizing your learning time for the vast amount of knowledge that might be right there, in your team.

Time well spent

I am sometimes lazy, and a pair drags me out of this comfort zone that I'm in. When pairing, you often feel a bit obliged to be there in terms of your full body and soul, so you don't have any phones, messages, chats, emails, or other side activities. In my personal experience, it is a good type of obligation – the one that gets me out of a state where I'm not very productive.

When in this state, I often feel really productive while pairing, compared to what I was doing just by myself. And that feeling is real and can be doubled by metrics. That is, if we count just the time spent versus the tasks that get completed, while forgetting about the better quality while pairing.

Often, I hear the following idea: *how can two people work on the same task?* It's absurd to lose the time of two people because you will produce just half the work! But things are more complicated than this, and not always *1+1 = 2*, especially when we're dealing with people.

Think of pair programming as a catalyzer that makes the whole reaction a lot more effective. If we make the whole experience of pair programming a nice and attractive one, we will have larger benefits than if people were to work alone, by themselves.

Summary

Pair programming can improve the whole development process of an organization significantly if it's implemented right. You can have a more enjoyable work environment while you're working closer to your peers. Pair programming is a practice that can reduce code defects, by letting more eyes see the code from an earlier start, and thus helps solve defects sooner and in a cheaper way. Also, because more people look at the code, the end product will be code that is easier to read, easier to understand, and, in conclusion, less prone to defects for future programmers who will change it.

If you haven't experienced the real power of pair programming, now is the time to continue reading and learn how you and your team can benefit from it. Furthermore, you can try remote pair programming, which is the same as pair programming, but it entails using a few different tools and there being a slightly different experience than doing pair programming in person.

It's never too late to start pair programming. I often paired with people who had at least double my experience, and they were pairing for the first time. If conducted well, the first pair programming session can open the eyes and hearts of any software professional.

In the beginning, it might be tiring, feel tedious, or be plain weird because now you need to explain your code to someone, often a stranger. But after a while, as with any learning curve, it will become easier, and you will feel the benefits.

So, I invite you to read further on how to try and succeed with remote pair programming in your organization. In the next chapter, we will look at how pair programming can help a team learn faster, either from each other or from someone outside the team.

Further reading

- *The Effective Executive*, by Peter Drucker (1966)

- *Introducing Staff Liquidity (1 of n)*, by Chris Matts: `https://theitriskmanager.com/2013/11/24/introducing-staff-liquidity-1-of-n`

- *Code review*: `https://en.wikipedia.org/wiki/Code_review`

- A curated list of articles, tools, books, and other resources on code review: `https://github.com/joho/awesome-code-review`

- *Teddy Bear Pair Programming*, by Adrian Bolboaca: `https://blog.adrianbolboaca.ro/2012/12/teddy-bear-pair-programming/`

2
How Can Pair Programming Help?

Pair programming can be useful in many ways, as we saw in the previous chapter, and in this chapter, we will look at how it can be helpful. There are also situations where pair programming can be challenging to use, or even not that effective, so we'll spend some time discovering that as well.

Pair programming can boost your overall efficiency, if done right. This is one of the top topics to discuss, especially with management, as it's counterintuitive to say that having five pairs working increases your overall efficiency compared to having 10 people working by themselves.

We will also discuss how pair programming can be helpful. There are many concrete ways in which pair programming is a good idea: better efficiency, improve technical skills, knowledge transfer, improve communication, increased problem-solving capabilities, or to simplify the existing code base. Also, there are situations where pair programming can be difficult, including working alone, lack of safe space, or being the only one who wants to pair from your team.

In this chapter, we're going to cover the following main topics:

- Defining pair programming
- Boosting team efficiency
- Situations where pair programming is useful
- Situations where pair programming is difficult
- Working better with colleagues with other specializations

Defining pair programming

When we are writing code, we are used to being alone, in front of a computer. As you saw in the previous chapter, we can also work in a different way, not just alone. In order to work together, we need to define pair programing and the roles associated with it.

This section will focus on the roles (or call them hats) of pair programming, namely *driver* and *navigator*. You might also have the role of a *trainer* or *facilitator* when you're doing this for the first time. Let's see what each of these roles entails.

Driver

The **driver** is the one who will have their hands on the keyboard and be writing the code. All the implementation details are at the latitude of the driver. Small decisions such as what type of variable to use, which programming language construct to use, how to name variables, methods, functions, classes, packages, and so on are a part of the driver's role.

The driver usually explains to the navigator what they are doing at all times. The purpose is dual: to clarify to themselves that they are doing the right thing and to explain to the driver what their intentions are. Cognitive science shows that when you explain something out loud, you clarify the topic to yourself as well. You will learn more about that in the next chapter.

The driver's role can be inverted with the navigator's role when the pairs consider it useful for their coding efficiency. For example, when the area of the code is well-known to the current navigator, but not that well-known to the current driver, they can decide to change *hats* so that the navigator becomes the driver and vice versa.

Navigator

The **navigator** will have their eyes on the screen and focus on all the long-term decisions. All the design and architecture details are at the latitude of the navigator, and the navigator will put discuss any implementation details that don't fit a coherent design or architecture.

The navigator will ask questions related to the current implementation, to understand if it affects the long-term decisions. Often, these questions get into deeper discussions about doing certain things. The driver and the navigator stop to discuss options and choose the best option for the given context.

Trainer/facilitator

A trainer is not synonymous with a facilitator, but you might have any of these two roles at one time in the organization.

A **trainer** will organize a learning activity by thinking about the learning outcomes, a participant's current skills, learning activities, duration, learning progression, and so on, and will then create a tentative program while considering all these factors. The trainer is heavily involved in most activities and plays a big role in directing the whole learning experience while explaining, demonstrating, and helping the group with hands-on activities.

The trainer is not an attendee but can join in with the activities to demonstrate how things can be done. Especially in the beginning with pair programming, it's useful that the trainer gets involved hands-on and writes code as a regular pair for a while.

At school, all of us went through training. There was a math teacher who explained how to compute the area of a triangle, then made a few exercises to show this, and then asked you and your classmates to do these exercises. Repetition is the mother of learning, as they say. That's the basic role of a trainer: to provide a clear agenda and clear scope with a clear level of difficulty, depending on the group.

A **facilitator** makes the whole activity easier for the group. The facilitator is not a regular participant, since the facilitator always needs to set the rules of the space for the participants and then enforce them.

The facilitator is not a moderator, nor a dictator. A good facilitator is the mirror image of the group – they manage to enforce the rules of the event by using the appropriate communication skills. The facilitator is also the steward of the event for the organizers or sponsors. All in all, the facilitator is a servant leader who requires excellent skills.

While a trainer is very involved and directs the group, the facilitator is there to set the rules and suggest alternatives to the group. The trainer gives direction, while the facilitator is much more flexible, often leaving the group to fail with the intention of using experiential learning.

Experiential learning means that we prefer to learn through our experiences, practicing and learning some topic at the same time. Under expert supervision, experiential learning is very effective and becomes more and more the basic method for educational systems worldwide. Difficult topics seem to be taught easier and faster with experiential learning.

When in school, if you were at a summer camp or at a scout camp, you had people who took care of you: guides, older students, teachers, and so on. They are the facilitators of that group. They are there to set the rules and create boundaries, with the main purpose to create a safe learning-oriented environment. At scout camps, the guides would put you in situations where you had to learn yourself: get a book of plants and then identify them in the forest, and then take pictures; then, whoever identifies the most plants wins a big prize.

So, the difference between a trainer and a facilitator is a big one. While the trainer has a clear agenda and teaches through the show-tell-guide-repeat method, the facilitator adapts to the context and creates a self-learning experience in a safe space.

Pair programming is simple: you have a driver and a navigator. They work together with different hats: the driver takes the small details, while the navigator looks beyond, further away. It's a good practice to start pair programming with a trainer and/or facilitator as it will boost your productivity by making it faster and simpler, with less time wasted. Time is money after all. Now, let's look at the ways in which efficiency can be boosted.

Boosting efficiency

Our mind sometimes plays tricks on us. We feel like we are making good progress and going in the right direction, but if we were to take a break for a moment, we would see that what we are doing is wrong. It's natural to have these types of experiences, which are not necessarily pleasant.

The key to improving our effectiveness is, believe it or not, to distance ourselves from the problem. Take breaks, take a walk, let your mind wander somewhere else. We say that we are thinking with a clear mind. Well, less task switching and taking breaks clears our minds.

Reducing task switching

First, let's learn what task switching is and why it can be bad – or most of the time, a really bad idea. Your brain, like a computer processor, can only focus on one intellectual activity at a time. If we do more things, such as driving and speaking on the phone, the brain splits its time between these two activities, like a computer processor. When we need to be focused on the road because we're driving on a busy intersection, or there's ice on the road, suddenly, we find that we didn't hear what the person on the phone was saying. In moments of physical danger, the brain will switch to the more important activity. Psychologists call the moments when the brain moves from one activity to another, task switching.

Imagine that you are completing basic tasks and talking to your colleague. You can do this as it's easy to do both activities at once. The cost of task switching isn't that big. Now, imagine you are doing a difficult, new type of task and you're trying to speak to your colleague. Suddenly, it will be very difficult to get the words out of your mouth, and very difficult to listen to what your colleague is saying. Furthermore, you will be extremely tired if you try to do these two tasks at once. By forcing the brain to do these two tasks, you become more tired, and you will feel the fatigue when you stop at the end of the day, later in the evening.

I know many people who take pride in doing many things at a time, such as chatting with the team, writing an email, watching a YouTube video, and engaging in conversations with nearby colleagues. That's a usual day at the office for some people. They feel like they are being productive and that they have done a lot. But, in fact, studies show us that at the end of the day, a person who would have done each of those activities one after the other would have been more productive, and would have been a lot less tired.

It may sound weird but working in a pair can generate more focus and fewer interruptions. We often feel that, by multitasking, we get a lot of things done. We may think that we are very efficient when we do many things at the same time, but we are actually being very inefficient.

There are multiple studies that show how multitasking affects efficiency, and the truth is that we can only multitask efficiently on very simple tasks. Programming is almost never a simple task. In fact, what happens in our brain is task switching; we never really multitask: our brain switches really fast from one task to another. The effects of task switching are the perception of personal efficiency, fatigue, and less efficient memory.

When we do pair programming, we focus on the task at hand. We have fewer interruptions from text chats, emails, impromptu discussions with colleagues, and so on. Because of that, we do less task switching – it may even be reduced to none in some instances. At the end of the day, we feel like there is this perception of fewer things getting done (compared to task switching, where we feel like we have done many things). But if we measure this, it's obvious that we do more things when we're pair programming.

The topic of task switching (or multitasking) often generates debate. This happens because we feel we are more productive when we have many things to do. We can draw the best conclusion by performing a simple experiment: we can measure how much we have done by task switching for, let's say, a week, and then measure the next week by how much we have done by completing focused, sequential tasks using the *Pomodoro Technique* (we will talk about this in the next section). In the third week, we can work in a pair and see how much work we have done. Measuring the results for all three situations would give us and our team the answer to this debate.

I can say that, in my context, all these theories apply: task switching only works for simple tasks; I am a lot more effective when pairing with someone than when working alone. This doesn't necessarily apply to everyone, but the general aspects apply.

Taking breaks

Another effect of pair programming is that we can take regular breaks. Otherwise, when working alone, it may happen that we work, and work, and work, until we look out the window and see it's already evening. We have no breaks, sometimes no lunch, and we don't even know where the time went.

This way of working can be very effective in the short term, but it can easily transform into fatigue, frustration, and, in some cases, depression.

When working in a pair, you are often forced to take breaks. And taking breaks comes with looking at the given task from another point of view. You can gain new perspectives, just because you detach from the problem for a few minutes.

A good practice is to use the **Pomodoro Technique** for time management. This technique was invented by the Italian psychologist Francesco Cirillo, and it's based on some studies that show that we can focus, on average, for 25 minutes. The technique is very simple and includes the following steps:

1. Choose a task.
2. Set the timer to a duration (usually 25 minutes).
3. Work on the given task.

4. When the timer rings, stop working and take a break (usually 5 minutes).

5. After 3-4 Pomodoros (task intervals), take a longer break (usually 15-30 minutes).

Using pair programming with Pomodoro is a very effective practice. Usually, pairing for a long period of time, plus using the Pomodoro Technique for time management, generates behavioral changes toward more sustainable ways of working.

Taking breaks is often considered, in classical project management or even in management, as *slacking*. People who have never done programming, testing, or any job in software development imagine that we can work like robots, without taking any breaks. The truth is that when we talk about knowledge work, we work with our brain, and almost always need to come up with innovative solutions and complex solutions that make us tired. Even if we don't feel it, we are tired and we need to take breaks for our success and for the project's success.

An unexpected outcome of pair programming is that we take more breaks and that we are more organized in our work.

To boost our efficiency, we need to be a bit more organized and deliberate with what we are doing. It may not seem difficult to some of you, but for many people, it is. From my experience, I can say that sometimes, being organized is easy, but when a lot of varied tasks come to me, I start being edgy, less organized, and more error-prone. That is when you should take larger and longer breaks: when in the heat of the moment when you are busy and pressured from all sides. So, my advice to you is, the busier you are, the more breaks you should take.

Now, let's explore some situations where pair programming can be helpful.

Situations when pair programming can help

There are multiple ways in which you can use pair programming to help you. As always, we need to make a decision about what we want to optimize. We can use pair programming for different purposes, and hence it's important to have a clear understanding as to what we want to use pair programming for during the coming period from the beginning.

In this section, we are going to cover some typical situations in which you can use pair programming. Note that some of them have opposite effects and cannot be used at the same time. That is why you need to choose consciously.

Bettering efficiency

Whenever a new feature is created, it will soon need our attention. This is important, even critical to the success of our software. There are these situations where we know we will work on an important, critical feature, and we need to prepare. When more complexity is involved, more eyes on the topic will create better solutions. So, in this situation, when we need to produce more, with more efficiency, pair programming helps a lot. It can sound counterintuitive that we can increase the efficiency by having five pairs working instead of 10 people working. Let's see why this happens.

Let's say that for a 1-day programming task, we need 2 hours of manual testing. If we find a defect or even a suggestion for improvement because of some unclear workflow or because of user experience, then we have 2 hours more for programming, and then another 2 hours for testing. Considering that we have this cycle twice, we have a total of 2 days of programming and 1 day of testing. To sum it up, we have 3 days of work.

How can pair programming help, then? Let's say the programmer works with another programmer, and the defect is spotted from the beginning. Here, the tester will use 2 hours to validate the solution. But of course, not everything can be observed from the beginning by programmers, which is why we have testers. To overcome that the programmer will pair for 1 hour with the tester as well, during the same initial first day of programming work. When we add things up, the initial scenario of 3 days of work transforms into 1 and a half days of cumulative teamwork. Overall, we are now more efficient, even if pairing with a tester cannot guarantee we catch all the defects.

We can object by saying that we will be slower when we pair with someone, so we need to explain what we are doing and we must discuss more so that we don't have the same speed. That is absolutely right. You can add some time so that you end up having 2 days' worth of work.

On the contrary, you can object and say that when you work in a pair, you need to stay focused. Social networks, chats, emails, the latest news, and other distractions are a lot less frequent. In this way, you increase your efficiency. By doing this, you probably end up with 1 and a half days of work again, considering the efficiency caused by eliminating distractions.

To conclude, if you are pressed for time and you need good quality (I'm sure everyone needs good quality, always!), pair programming done right, with a focus on collaboration, will bring you faster to results than solo programming.

Improving technical skills

As a programmer, we need to constantly improve our technical skills. We live in a knowledge world where everything changes and new things appear often, so to keep up, we always need to keep improving. You can always join a workshop to learn the theory for a new topic or join an online learning program to find out how to use the new technology, but you also need to use the new topic, the new practice, or the new technology in practice. In terms of practice, it is a lot better to have a pair. Pair programming can be used with great efficiency to learn, practice, and improve technical skills.

One recommended way to use pair programming to improve skills is to allocate some weekly learning time for the pair. Depending on urgency, topic, difficulty, and other aspects, you need to allocate more or less time for learning.

A good approach is to have an organizer (team leader, scrum master, any team member) who will take care that everything that is appropriate for learning (invite everyone in the calendar, have a room, and so on), and who will remind everyone about the learning time if needed. The organizer doesn't have any special role in the overall learning process. It's just a simple, temporary role to make sure that everyone is on the same page and that learning can happen.

Of course, you can also improve technical skills without having an organized team learning format with pair programming. You can use pair programming when you're learning new topics by yourself. Just find one or more colleagues who are interested in the same topic and pair with them every once in a while to improve your technical skills.

I am a strong believer in deliberate learning methods. Deliberate learning means that you know what you know well, and what you need to improve. You make it your job to learn, and then keep learning continuously. Because we are talking about programming, we need to learn through practice, and the best form of deliberate learning is to practice together with other passionate peers.

Aiding knowledge transfer

We need to transfer some technical and/or domain knowledge from our more experienced team members to new team members. The experience doesn't necessarily mean senior to junior. It may also mean from a senior to another senior, but we refer to certain topics where not all the knowledge is aligned in the team.

As we talk about programming, it's difficult to have knowledge transfer without getting your hands into the code. Writing code in a specific context is essential for learning. In such a situation, pair programming fits like a glove.

Usually, the more *experienced person* would be the *driver*, and the *trainee* would be the *navigator*. The driver starts with the basics, explains what needs to be done, continues with some coding, and the navigator takes notes. Then, the navigator needs to do the same steps for a task alone, and then figures out that it's more difficult than it seemed. Then, they go back to their colleague who was acting as the driver and start asking questions. That's what I would call non-experiential learning, for the lack of a better term.

A better approach is to have the less experienced person be the driver, and the more experienced person be the navigator. After a short introduction, where the more experienced person explains the basics, the theory, and how things work, the navigator tries doing things. Of course, it will start off feeling a little clumsy for the navigator, and they'll make all sorts of beginner's mistakes, or do silly things. But this is all normal when you are learning something. With this approach, the navigator needs to, well, navigate. The navigator would rather give instructions about what to do, rather than giving precise implementation details, such as spelling all the commands. It might feel like a struggle for the trainee, at least in the beginning, but it's a lot more effective. When the trainee takes on a new task that needs the new topic, it's a lot easier to do things alone. Of course, questions might arise, and this is normal, but overall, things will be a lot clearer for the trainee by the end of the activity.

While the driver does things with their own hands, it's easier to remember what to do and what mistakes not to repeat. Having an experienced person nearby that can guide the trainee out of obvious traps is useful for a smoother learning experience. All in all, it's a more frustrating learning experience, but it's a more effective way for your time to be spent.

The driver in the second situation needs to keep their calm, expect to be frustrated in the beginning, and expect to pass through a learning curve. Of course, that learning curve can be more or less steep. It depends on the topic, their overall knowledge, their willingness to learn, and many other factors.

The navigator in the second situation needs to remain in the role of a guide – no complex explanations about how things work in the background, no unnecessary details, no derogatory comments about the speed of doing things, or any other actions of that sort. As an experienced person, you need to have the patience and willingness to wait until all is clear for the trainee.

All the aspects we just discussed are very important for efficient experiential learning sessions. Communication is a big part of the whole experience. Pair programming has an inherently built-in communication component that the more experienced person needs to master, for an efficient and pleasant learning experience.

Improving communication

Usually, a team coach, team leader, or manager can observe, after spending some time with the team, when a team is not communicating well. A well-functioning team will talk in a low tone, having clear discussions about the pros or cons of an idea, taking care to understand the other person's views, and always taking time to explain as many times as it's necessary.

We can observe when we need to improve the way we communicate with each other. Way too often we may be too aggressive, abrasive, and don't listen enough to others. This behavior leads to less collaboration inside the team. A team member who may have to face aggression, unjust criticism, or blame would prefer to stay further away from the team activities and will feel trapped inside the team and during the team meetings.

It might seem surprising that we talk about communication when dealing with pair programming. This topic feels more like a psychological one, or a soft skills topic, rather than something you would fix with pair programming. It's true that pair programming is not a fix for this situation, but without improving communication, pair programming will probably not work.

Going back to how a well-functioning team needs to communicate, there is some general advice that is useful both when attending a meeting and when pairing:

- Use assertive communication when expressing positive and negative ideas by being open, direct, and honest while giving clear reasoning for your views.

- Use nonviolent communication when giving feedback, expressing your views, or expressing criticism about a given context and situation.

- Learn from Clean Language how to express your intention clearly, without leaving many assumptions about what you expressed.

Let's go through a brief explanation of the concept of nonviolent communication. The whole system was created by Marshal Rosenberg, a psychologist who, for many years, studied how violence affects our communication, in conjunction with Mahatma Gandhi's nonviolent revolution from India. Nonviolent communication is a whole system that explains how to stop pushing us to have obligations, meaning things we believe we can't avoid, and how to stop being violent while communicating with the others. It's a great concept, and I recommend the book *Nonviolent Communication*, written by Marshal Rosenberg.

Clean Language is a communication method developed by psychologist David J Grove, and it was used for many years just in clinical therapy and counseling. After a while, it started being used in coaching, and now, we see it being used more and more in management as well, passed from management coaches. The subset of Clean Language that we can use is related to understanding the importance of words, their meaning, and the symbolistic and metaphors that we use in verbal communication. It's a very good technique for asking questions without interfering too much, if any, with the answer.

All of this is just some general advice. Going into too much detail is beyond the scope of this book. I recommend that you find other resources, training, or coaching to improve your and your team's communication skills. There are some pair programming games I often use that focus on communication. In fact, many of the pair programming learning activities I usually use are focused on improving the communication inside the team. There are some useful activities such as *Beginner's Mind*, *Yes*, and *Silent Programming*, and many others that use pair programming to improve the communication skills of the pair. We will talk about how to use these techniques for remote pair programming in more detail in the following chapters.

When we work in a team, it's important to focus on good communication. We cannot have good collaboration without good communication. And we cannot have good pair programming without good communication.

Enhancing problem-solving capabilities

We need to expand our knowledge base for solutions that can seem exotic and unusual compared to what we were used to. The reason for trying these types of solutions is that we can write less code for more features. It may sound counterintuitive, but writing less code is a lot harder than writing more code. And if we add the clarity aspect to the code we write, the whole process becomes even more difficult.

A good technique for finding more innovative solutions is using *lateral thinking*. We can define lateral thinking as solving problems by viewing them using a different, creative approach. There are some typical challenges to getting to grips with what lateral thinking is. From time to time, I like to take lateral thinking challenges unrelated to software development. This is a good approach to exercising lateral thinking, and it will help you find solutions faster in the software development world as well. It's exercise for your brain. This exercise can be beneficial for all life situations.

Why do we want to use lateral thinking? The reason is simple: we want everyone in the team to be used to thinking and coming up with solutions, rather than saying "*we have always done it like that.*" It can happen that many of these solutions are not great, but sometimes, we may end up with a great idea – a jewel.

Pair programming can catalyze such problem-solving capabilities because the pairs can exchange ideas back and forth on how to proceed. If we are open to new ideas, we try to iteratively improve a rough idea, and we often have something great at hand. The pairs who know the context will generate far better solutions and come up with faster coding and faster feature development.

I will emphasize the importance of having this *playground*, where programmers can try out things, iterate on them, and then validate or invalidate ideas and solutions. With pair programming, you can do this; the only restrictions are usually artificial constraints decided on by the organization or by the overall environment. Restrictions such as "*only the senior comes with the design,*" or "*use blindly what the architect said,*" or "*don't use pair programming more than 1 hour per day*" will not be beneficial for the overall quality of the solutions.

We often like to program *elegant* solutions – those solutions that fit the context really well, the business domain, are easy to understand and easy to change. But these solutions never come easy, and never come out in one go. We iterate on such solutions, come up with an idea, and then pair program, often with different people, in order to shape them better and polish them until we have something great.

Pair programming and collaboration go hand-in-hand when we want to increase the problem-solving capabilities of a software development team.

Simplifying the existing code base

While coding, we need to look back at our current code base and simplify it, because we may have introduced too much accidental complexity; it now becomes too complex for what it's doing.

I have heard so many times from teams that their code base is difficult to understand, that they are afraid to change parts of it, or it takes too much time just to change one very simple thing. Some people call that **technical debt**: an accumulation of badly written code because we had tight deadlines, we cut corners, or we didn't take the time to refactor.

Often, it's scary to be alone out there in the wild. Having a pair helps a lot with having a bit more courage, because you have someone by your side.

Also, you can make very good progress when you think about who should be in the pairs. You should look at the current skills and knowledge of the team and choose complementary skills that will make solving the problem or simplifying the code a faster task. You can have pairs such as the following:

- A programmer who knows the domain and a programmer who knows refactoring well

- A programmer and a tester

- An analyst and a programmer

By doing this, it's less like that they make mistakes that are obvious from a coding or domain point of view. Of course, the code should still pass through a code review, or more pairing sessions with other specialists, to make sure the simplification makes sense and respects all the guidelines.

It's always a good idea to have more pairs of eyes when you're working on the existing code. While thinking about the complexity of the existing code, even if you really know the business logic, the programming language, and the environment, you can still make mistakes. The reason for making mistakes is because there are so many moving parts, and our brain simply cannot grasp all the implications of a small change.

Due to this, using pair programming makes sense when you're looking at existing code base s. The implications of making small changes can have an unexpected impact, but by using pair programming, you can minimize the probability of making mistakes.

As you can see, pair programming has many effects on your team, organization, and every person. It's a practice that helps you improve technical, communication, and problems solving skills. One of the main reasons pair programming can be so effective is that if it's done right, it can help on so many levels.

Now, let's look at some situations where pair programming can be inconvenient for some.

Situations when pair programming is difficult

Pair programming is not just cookies, candies, and sweets all the time. It can also become a bitter experience in some situations. We shouldn't force anyone to use pair programming, as it's not for everybody. It's a good practice, a good tool, but as with anything, there are exceptions. Let's see some typical situations where pair programming is difficult to use, or where it shouldn't be used at all.

Working alone

There are people who like working alone and who are efficient in doing so. For them, collaboration is difficult, and going to meetings seems like a waste of time. For these people, pair programming is really difficult, and we need to check if it is a good idea to bring them onto the pair programming bandwagon.

It might be debatable if such a programmer has a place in the team. Regular team players might think that such a person should be fired because they don't play by the team rules. On the other hand, such people can be really productive in areas they like or know when working on their own. Only if such a person is very unhappy or unproductive working as a pair does it makes sense to see if working alone produces good results for them or the team.

In my experience, I have worked with such people who were great, and were always supportive of their team, even if they were working alone. On the other hand, I have also seen some who were counterproductive to the team.

Previously, we mentioned the hypothesis that pair programming can boost efficiency, and that it can be an investment for you and your team. However, pair programming can be counterproductive for some who prefer working alone. They may feel like it's making them slower, it's cumbersome, that they need to socialize and talk to their colleagues, and so on. The truth, however, is that it's sometimes good to go slower and increase the quality of your job.

Often, you need to put a lot of energy into pairing with a work-alone style of developer. Trying this may create some tension in the team, and often, a lot of stress for the one who loves working solo. Due to this, it's tricky to say that pair programming will work for developers who enjoy working solo. You need a lot of tact and a lot of time just to try it.

Lack of safe space

In software development or engineering, we always need to come up with solutions for difficult problems, or at least for problems we haven't dealt with before. Because of this, we need to brainstorm solutions and bounce off ideas within the team. When brainstorming, we can come up with crazy ideas, or ideas that might sound crazy in the beginning, but with a bit of polishing can be something great.

Having a safe space means having this environment where all the team members can come with their so-called crazy ideas without being ridiculed, mocked, or laughed at. A safe space means that no idea is bad, any idea can be taken into account, and any idea can be considered for use by the team.

Having a safe space for learning and brainstorming ideas is essential for a good software development environment, and, of course, for a pair programming environment.

Pair programming is difficult when you don't have this safe space. It's almost impossible to bounce off ideas and try new things without the openness that the safe space offers.

Only I want to pair from my team

Maybe many of you have been in this situation where only you want to adopt a certain practice, and your team doesn't want to hear about it. I know I have been in this situation, and I can tell you it's not easy.

Let's say you want to try pair programming with your team, and they don't. The best thing you can do is try to convince at least one of your colleagues. Don't try to convince everyone, because it will be very difficult.

When you have convinced one person, try to make the most out of it. Don't push it to the limits, such as by pairing the whole day. Try to show that you two can work a lot faster than your colleagues expect. Show that it's not only a learning or efficiency opportunity, but it's also a time of having fun and enjoyment. After your colleagues see that it works well, they might reconsider their opinion. Usually, you will see a few of them saying that they want to try pair programming as well. From then on, if you continue, things will only get easier.

You might have a few colleagues who will not want to pair at all. That's fine; just leave them to code by themselves. There's no reason in trying to convince everyone. If it works for most of the team, you have already done something great by convincing most of them.

In the least favorable case for pair programming, you cannot convince anyone to pair. This can happen, and the only thing I can recommend is to try pair programming with other peers outside your team. Pair on pet projects or open source projects. Alternatively, you can try remote pair programming with people you don't know.

As you can see, a safe space is a prerequisite for using pair programming. Otherwise, it can produce more harm than good. Also, there are people who work very well alone, with less collaboration, and with less contact with their team, and we should understand them and create a context for them so that they're as effective as they can be in their own terms.

Working better with colleagues with other specializations

Pair programming can be extended to more than just programmers. I have paired successfully with people with many skills and those with different specializations. It's great to understand their angle and their point of view, and all this knowledge can help you become a better professional.

I look at pairing with professionals from other specializations as a win-win situation. Both pairs learn something. You need to have correct expectations and a good setup to make the magic happen.

In this section, we will look at typical situations where different specialists can pair in the same team. We will learn how to approach these mixed pairing scenarios as we drift slowly from pair programming to generic pairing. We will focus on a higher level than programming by looking at the product we are building from more aspects: testing, user experience, operations, business, and so on.

Pairing with a tester

There are several flavors of pairing with a tester. Let's look at a few of these usual flavors and how each can help you understand the testing activities better.

Probably the most frequent situation is when you have a defect, and the tester shows you how to replicate the defect. It's interesting to see the steps, the flow, and the reasoning behind a flow showing the defect. You can learn how to try and replicate a defect on your own, or how to test your code as a programmer, before you can say that you're done coding.

Another frequent situation is when you pair with a tester with the purpose of automating some checks. When I first paired with a tester for this purpose, I found the whole process really amazing. I learned so much about a test plan, how to think about which checks needed to be automated, how to automate those chosen checks, and so many other things. The tester learned how to write better, more expressive code, and how to structure the classes and methods so that they were maintainable.

Maybe the least frequent situation is when you have a tester who does exploratory testing through pair programming. Let's say that you constantly review your code while it's written. And the tester tells you in an instant if the code you just wrote might generate an issue. The tester explores the code while it's being produced. You cannot get faster feedback than that! The tester learns more about writing code, some design intricacies, and how a programmer thinks while writing code. Even if it sounds weird in the beginning, I do recommend that you take the first opportunity to pair with a tester who has such skills for exploratory testing. Keep an open mind and trust me – you will learn so much!

Pairing with a UI designer

UI designers have a really good view of how things need to look and feel. I, as a programmer, can say that the UI interfaces I have created myself are clunky and need a lot of improvement.

Pairing with a designer gives you more appreciation for the finer details and angles from which a UI interface needs to experienced. A programmer can definitely learn the patience of getting every pixel done right, and also the patience of testing the UI on several screen dimensions, color schemes, or through various accessibility contexts.

Usually, UI designers know how to code, but pairing with someone who codes all day long can be beneficial. You, as a programmer, can teach a UI designer about structuring the code, naming it, optimizing the code for reliability, reusability, and all in all how to have nice, clean code, the same as having a nice clean UI interface.

Pairing with DevOps

It's always a good opportunity to learn how to think about a system in terms of keeping it alive in terms of its deployment, performance, and monitoring. You, as a programmer, can pair on writing scripts to automate all these things, or create tools that help the team with the automation pipeline.

It's a good opportunity to gain an operational point of view, while also being a good opportunity to learn how to write better, easier to maintain code for the other side. Since DevOps is a mix between development and operations, we have people who have done operations, or people who have done development, in the past. People who have done operations would benefit from pairing with a programmer by learning how to organize their scripts, their code, and how to have a good design for reusability and clarity.

Pairing with a business analyst

You can learn a lot of interesting details about a complex business domain when pairing with a business analyst. Also, it's interesting to learn how to deconstruct a difficult feature into small parts, look into all the details, and ask questions about all the implications. Usually, pairing with a business analyst improves the analysis skills of any programmer. I've learned a lot from business analysts and testers about how to look at a problem, and how to formulate possible solutions.

Many analysts like seeing how their analysis turns into code. Some of them program as well, so they like to see how a professional gets things done.

Often, while pairing, the programmer has a similar experience as when pairing with a tester and getting the fastest possible feedback. In a few seconds, you can find out if your logic is good and whether the names of your variables, classes, methods, functions, or namespaces are good. You learn so much about having clarity in your code, so I always find pairing with business analysts invaluable.

Don't stop with just the roles that I have mentioned in this section. These are the most usual examples of roles you can find in a software team. Go out there and pair with anyone who wants to, not caring too much about their role or expertise in the organization.

In the next section, we'll learn how pair programming can look in practice, and how it can help.

Pair programming in practice

I am usually very keen on pairing with varied people, as I know I will learn so many small things that will add up and make me a better professional. In this section, we will look at how being open to new challenges and being social can lead to a fast and almost continuous learning experience in the long term.

Learning new things or tricks

I think that we all need to learn continuously as we are part of an industry where so many things change, often with such incredible speed. Because I wanted to learn as effectively as possible, I tried many types of learning formats. After trying many options, over time, I can say that my favorite type of learning is by pairing. For me, it's a form of accelerated learning. Pair programming is an excellent opportunity for learning, irrespective of domain, role, or level in an organization.

In my case, I learned many small tips and tricks on how to use a programming language, a library, an IDE, or just how to approach a certain situation. Every small detail about how every one of my pairs approaches a given problem is an opportunity for learning. The key is to pair with many people, to learn many new small things from each of them.

If you pair with colleagues or team members daily, you will see a lot of interesting things, including small tips, tricks, and hacks that your colleagues do. As time goes by, you will learn less and less or even risk getting into a rut, where you and your colleagues don't see many alternative ways or improvement methods for your current ways.

Pairing often with people you don't work with regularly is a great option to keep up the learning process. It's rather easy to use remote pair programming with people you know, you don't work often with, or even with people you don't know.

Being social – social programming

Social programming is an idea that stresses the fact that we also need a community and people around us, not just computers, screens, and keyboards. Social programming means that we actively try to find people to learn new topics and ideas from, to stay up to date. Pair programming is a flavor of social programming.

It's true that maybe we are too often surrounded by computers and might forget about the human side of things. We build software products for people, for real users, for businesses that are made up of people, who, in turn, sell their products to people. By focusing so much on the technical things, such as coding, architecture, design, programming languages, frameworks, editors, deployments, and so on, we might forget that programming is done for people.

It's a good idea to open up more to people and, at least for a while, forget about all the technical stuff. You can pair with people who have no clue about programming. I have done so in various situations. For them, you look like a sorcerer who can make things happen, and they understand what work you need to do to add a simple button to the screen.

So, pair with anyone non-technical as well. It can be anyone in your team, or in your organization that has the openness to do so. I have paired with product owners, project managers, directors, and even board members or CEOs. It can sound intimidating, but just do what you normally do, and you will observe a better connection with them after a few of these sessions.

Pair programming cannot solve everything

Until now, I have rather praised pair programming. But like any tool and any practice, there are situations where pair programming won't work or solve anything. Let's look at some usual situations.

Unclear requirements

There's a saying in software development: junk in, junk out. When you have unclear requirements, the obvious pain is not improving your production tools or practices, such as learning how to use pair programming. And pair programming will not help at all with unclear requirements.

The alternative is to have good, high-quality requirements. But be careful: we don't need to get back to waterfall and linger for 1-2 years just to document everything. When talking about high-quality requirements, there needs to be a fine balance that we can define as the simplest, shortest requirement so that the team can get to work immediately, without asking for clarifications.

So, this concept of clear requirements is very context-dependent. There's one thing to write specifications for a difficult domain, and there's another thing to have a simple domain at hand. In any situation, you always need feedback from the team and adjust the quantity, form, and quality of the requirements, depending on what they need.

Bad coding practices

When there is pressure on getting things done, we often have bad coding practices. Pushing for a short deadline generates bad quality. Of course, there are many other alternatives to getting bad-quality code. No matter how you got there, pair programming won't help a lot with getting out of there.

The alternative is to create an environment where quality is the first criteria, and then understand what parts of the code need improving. Only after you start working on improving the code base does introducing pair programming become a good idea.

Tension within the team

Using pair programming to alleviate tensions in the team is not a good idea. I had contact with managers that had this idea: let's have a workshop, and let's start a new practice to make the team(s) happier.

When there are tensions in the team or the team members are not happy with various aspects of their professional life, a workshop or a practice will not help. First, we need to solve that issue, create a learning environment, and then continue with the first thing that is useful for the team(s).

Tension within the organization

Organizations get through rough changes sometimes, or there may be moments of great tension because of market changes, pushing tight deadlines, quality, security, or performance concerns. When you are in a tight spot like this, pair programming won't help. It's not a good idea to try and introduce a new practice.

In this moment, you should use all your energy to make the best effort possible to support the organization. Only try this when there is a foreseeable future to experiment with new tools, techniques, and ideas.

Close to deployment time

You may have the idea to start pair programming with the team close to a deployment or delivery time. But the problem is that focusing on learning a new tool or technique too close to a deployment date might generate the failure to deploy on time.

The best idea is to wait after the deployment and think of a plan to start using pair programming. A good moment to start any learning activity is a few weeks after a tiring and difficult experience, such as a deployment.

In conclusion, you need to find a good time to introduce a new practice such as pair programming. Quite often, I see people frustrated that they are trying to introduce a new practice at the wrong time, and the organization rejected it. This situation comes with a double difficulty: when you have tried something in a wrong way or at a wrong time, it is a lot more difficult to be open to trying it again.

Summary

In this chapter, we learned how to get in touch with pair programming and the best ways to get started with it. Since pair programming is a good tool for boosting efficiency, we saw how to get the most out of pair programming in our team or organization. We saw how pair programming can help, but also situations when pair programming is difficult or not recommended.

For a while, we got out of the programming context and extended pair programming to the other specializations as well. It's the whole team that pairs, and everyone can learn so much from each other. Being social, collaborating well, and being open to new ideas, tips, and tricks means that anyone can use pair programming as a continuous learning opportunity.

At the end of this chapter, we looked at the limitations of pair programming. We should not force any tool outside its purpose as we will waste time, or even worse, we will garner negative effects.

In the next chapter, we will be exploring different pair programming techniques and styles, along with the contexts in which they are the most effective.

Further reading

- *Facilitating Technical Events*, by Adrian Bolboacă
- *The Illusion of Multitasking Improves Performance on Simple Tasks*: `https://insights.som.yale.edu/insights/the-illusion-of-multitasking-improves-performance-on-simple-tasks`
- *Task switching*: `https://en.wikipedia.org/wiki/Task_switching_(psychology)`
- *Nonviolent Communication*, by Marshal Rosenberg
- A series of articles on *Pair Programming Games* by Adrian Bolboacă: `https://blog.adrianbolboaca.ro/category/pair-programming-games/`
- *No Silver Bullet: Essence and Accidents of Software Engineering*, by Frederick P. Brooks, Jr.

3
Exploring Pair Programming Techniques and Styles

In the previous chapter, we learned how useful pair programming can be. We discussed how pair programming can be used to reduce task switching, offer better technical results, provide faster knowledge transfer, and how it can improve overall communication. We will now examine how pair programming can be even better by using collaboration-style methods that are appropriate for a number of typical (usual) contexts.

In this chapter, you will learn about several pair programming techniques and styles and how to use each of them. These techniques and styles are useful as they provide a framework for using pair programming effectively.

One **pair programming technique** distinguishes itself from another by the way each of the two partners works together, how active or passive each one of them is, what the role of each pair is, and how often the roles between the two partners are switched.

A **pair programming style** is defined by the way the two partners interact with each other. The partners can be equally balanced, one of the partners can have a more active role, or one can even be in the center of the activity. However, remember that some pair programming styles are not compatible with some techniques, so watch out when you choose from any of them.

We need to use each of the pair programming techniques or styles in the appropriate context in order to obtain optimum results; and by results, I am referring to productivity, work enjoyment, and learning efficiency.

In this chapter, we will focus on the following topics:

- Understanding pair programming techniques
- Improving pair programming with styles
- Organizing pair programming
- How often do we need to pair?
- Exploring different communication methods
- Pair programming best practices
- Pair programming anti-patterns
- Boosting productivity with remote pair programming

Understanding pair programming techniques

There are several usual pair programming techniques that can be used for different purposes and with different effects. We will go into greater detail regarding the most popular pair programming techniques. Every technique has its place in a certain context. Additionally, it's useful to use some techniques in some cases and other techniques when the situation changes. We will discuss, in detail, when each of these techniques is useful.

Note that there is a generic setup that you need to take into account, no matter what technique you use: ensure that you have two keyboards, two mice, and a monitor at the same distance and angle for both partners. That is all; we will detail any additional requirements for each specific technique as we go further.

Most of the time, there is a rotation between the two partners. When using any of these techniques, both partners will have a specific focus. During a rotation, this focus changes between the partners. We will detail rotation specifics for each particular technique as well.

Each tool or technique also usually has its own set of advantages and disadvantages, and we will detail these as well. In order to be effective, it's not only important to choose the right tool for the job but to also know your tools from experience.

All of these techniques need to be practiced, understood, and can even be forgotten to the point where you just choose the appropriate one by following your instinct. These are detailed descriptions that have a didactical purpose and might not be complete, as it's difficult to include every angle without the reader getting bored or the author splitting hairs.

The Driver-Navigator technique

As the name suggests, in this technique, we have two people and two roles: the driver and the navigator. You can liken this technique to racing cars, where the driver holds the wheel and the navigator is expected to explain, upfront, the obstacles and dangers on the road.

The *driver* is the one writing the code and focusing on the small details. Ultimately, they are in charge and make all of the decisions.

The *navigator* observes the driver writing the code and focuses on the long-term decisions. Additionally, the navigator can suggest ideas, come up with alternative options, and show the potential risks, dangers, or fallbacks of the current code.

Setup

In this scenario, the driver keeps the keyboard and writes the code. The navigator doesn't require a keyboard but a second computer, where they can search for resources, find answers, refer to the relevant documentation, and more.

Rotation

When using this technique, rotations are done very seldom or not at all. To begin, try to switch roles after every finalized task, which can take from a few hours to a few days. After a few pair programming sessions, you can also begin switching within the same task.

Advantages

The advantages of this technique are as follows:

- Fewer, or no, rotations generate less context switching.
- The driver can focus on writing the code for a long time with the help of the navigator.

- For the navigator, this can be a useful learning context for better communication. Since the navigator can only suggest ideas, they need to be able to efficiently explain how short-term decisions will affect the long-term evolution.

Disadvantages

The disadvantages of this technique are as follows:

- Because of few or no rotations, it can be tiring for the driver to focus on writing the code. Bigger and more frequent breaks could help in this situation.

- It can be frustrating for the navigator to not be able to put their hands on the keyboard. However, as we mentioned earlier, this can also be an advantage learning-wise.

- This technique is not the most effective way of getting things done. Sometimes, the navigator suggests good ideas, but without communicating them well, the driver will continue with their own ideas.

When to use it

This style is useful when you are beginning to pair-program. It's useful to create a common way of doing things, with people adapting to one another. There is not much change from usual programming and because of that, it's easier to get started with it.

When I start pairing with someone new, I instinctively start with Driver-Navigator. It's my go-to starting approach. Then, I might adapt the technique, taking into consideration what my new pairing partner likes and what our task is going to be.

You can call Driver-Navigator the *snowball of advancing knowledge*. Once, I was pairing as an external consultant to teach different topics such as unit testing and dealing with legacy code. In this particular scenario, I was paired with Peter, an experienced programmer. I started by briefly explaining how I would like to pair. For the first hour or so, I wanted to balance the time between me and my pair, starting with Driver-Navigator but making sure that we rotate often enough to gain some momentum with the learning process. Usually, my new partners find it easier to start with Driver-Navigator: as I show how to write a unit test, they show the business and code details. For me and for my pair, it's a game of rolling a snowball, making the snowball bigger and bigger as we learn from each other during each rotation.

Remarks

The Driver-Navigator technique is, from many points of view, the opposite of Strong-Style pairing. Strong-Style pairing means that the driver is just a *smart* keyboard, and the navigator is extremely active and constantly explaining to the driver what to do. The name "Strong Style" comes from the fact that the navigator is strong in an unbalanced way, and the driver doesn't have much liberty. Strong-Style pairing can be described by inverting the roles that we just discussed in the Driver-Navigator technique. We will dive into more detail about Strong-Style pairing later on in this chapter.

Note that you can also have the driver be the beginner, and then the navigator takes on the role of an active technical coach. This first approach will generate more pressure on the beginner. That is why the navigator needs to have good coaching and training skills. Being able to explain things efficiently, going into detail about why to do certain things, and convincing the beginner to try something are all tools that need to be used here.

Alternatively, you can have the driver be the advanced one of the two, and the navigator will learn by watching the driver operate. This second approach can generate less pressure for the beginner, but it might result in fewer learning outcomes. Additionally, this second approach can become very difficult for the beginner if the driver works really rapidly without explaining much. While it would be useful to see, not much learning will take place during those hours of pairing.

The Pairing-Trainee technique

This technique is used to teach programmers how to start using pair programming. No matter the programming experience of the programmer, this technique works for adding this pair programming tool to the programmer's tool belt. It's important to increase the confidence of the trainee, so the trainer must behave in a gentle and open manner. This is so that they can build up the trainee's interest in coding as opposed to judging their current skills.

Setup

For this technique, it is helpful to have two keyboards, two mice, and two monitors. However, note that the trainee will drive most of the time. The second keyboard can be used by the trainer for short periods of time, just to show something small that is extremely useful in the context, such as a shortcut or a way to make the code elegant more quickly.

Rotation

For the first few sessions, we shouldn't rotate within this technique. The driver will always be the trainee.

After the first few pair programming sessions, we can start rotating once every 30 or 40 minutes and gradually decrease the time as needed. Because of the decrease in rotation time, we can then naturally introduce the Driver-Navigator technique.

Advantages

Advantages of this technique include the following:

- The most effective way to understand how easy and fast it is to use pair programming is by pairing with someone who is advanced in pair programming.

- While pairing with someone who has done this for a long time, you can learn tricks based on the current need, choose the best approaches, take breaks when necessary, and more.

Disadvantages

Disadvantages of this technique include the following:

- It might feel forced, or unnatural, at the beginning for the trainee. We need to address this potential issue straight away and be very open about future pairing sessions. Ask the trainees to voice all of their concerns upfront and then answer them. In this way, we can at least minimize this feeling of working in an awkward manner – something that they aren't used to doing.

- Initially, programmers might feel afraid that we will assess their skills and code and judge them based on this. In order to mitigate this risk, we need to remain friendly and explain, in depth, what we are going to do. More importantly, we need to reassure them that we are not assessing their technical skills or their code. Sometimes, people seem to think that when someone new comes and works with them, they will judge them. So, set the rules of the game straight from the beginning: we will work together to learn pair programming and no judgment or shaming will occur.

When to use it

This is a very good technique to use during the first few sessions of pair programming. Once the trainee pair-programmer has learned the movements of pair programming, this technique will no longer be useful and we can then move on to the Driver-Navigator technique. Only once the ideas behind how to pair, how to communicate, and how to work together in a pair are clearly understood, is it a good idea to switch to another pair programming technique.

In an organization where I was working as an external trainer, Iris was pairing with John. Iris was a senior programmer and John was a junior programmer. Iris was extremely experienced in pair programming and many other techniques. I spoke to Iris about how to approach the pairing session with John, and I explained to her the Pairing-Trainee technique. At the time, I was working with someone else, close to Iris and John, and was observing what was happening. John was almost full-time driving. Once, it so happened that Iris wanted to show John how to extract a method with the automated refactoring tool. Then, nearly half an hour later, Iris took the keyboard again to show him how to structure a class better so that it respects the team's coding standards. The rest of the time, Iris was very patient and calm, explaining to John how pair programming worked and working according to John's speed. Of course, with John being a junior programmer, his speed was much slower, but Iris didn't push him at all.

After their pairing session, which took around 70 minutes, I asked John how he felt. He said it was intensive, but he liked it because he was able to learn a lot and also learn from an experienced programmer who was very likable. Iris told me that it was challenging to keep such a low rhythm, but she understood its importance when being paired with a junior programmer.

Remarks

This technique is a good icebreaker into pair programming. This is because, quite often, starting directly with the Driver-Navigator technique can feel like too much to take in at once since there are so many rules and guidelines to follow. When teaching or learning something new, it's always a good idea to use a gradual approach and keep adding more difficult elements once the previous elements have been absorbed.

The Beginner-Advanced technique

This technique is about teaching a programming beginner a specific topic using pair programming. It's not to be mistaken with the previous technique of Pairing Trainee.

Setup

As usual, two keyboards, two mice, and two monitors make a good setup to begin with. Even if the driver is always a beginner, the navigator can point things out by showing something or writing for a brief period of time.

Rotation

To begin with, there are no rotations. For the first few sessions, the driver will always be the beginner. However, after a few sessions, we can introduce some rotations if the advanced programmer considers that learning will be more effective in this way.

Advantages

The most effective way to learn something new is by using pair programming. This technique leverages pair programming to allow you to teach and learn new skills, tools, and practices. In this scenario, the two partners are focused on what they need to do, and focused experiential learning is one of the best options when teaching someone something new.

Disadvantages

This technique might feel forced or unnatural at the beginning for the trainee. By managing expectations before starting the pairing sessions, these feelings of being forced will decrease. Additionally, a good approach is to explain, step by step, what will happen, how the pairing will take place, what its advantages are, and acknowledge that it will be extremely tiring.

When to use it

This is a method that I mostly use when I am being a technical coach, and I need to explain various tools or techniques to beginner programmers. The technique works very well when an experienced programmer, or a team leader, has a junior team member and the new team member needs to learn a lot of new tools, practices, and skills.

Programming is best learned by practicing it. And what better way to practice than with an experienced programmer by your side? You can get guidance from them when you make mistakes, and you can also see how other experienced programmers work.

After a training session, I always recommend what we call "training on the job." This means that we can apply our knowledge directly in production, on the code base of the trainee, and in the role of the trainee. Once, I was pairing, for the first time, with a junior programmer, George, at his desk. The pairing session followed a unit testing workshop that he had attended a week prior. We started by looking at his tasks for the near future, and then we agreed to work together on one of the tasks. As we had followed a workshop, I played the role of the teacher who asked George to apply again, in production code this time, the knowledge and practice acquired at the workshop. In this scenario, I'm observing, asking questions when I feel George's actions are unclear, and then assisting him when he gets stuck. When George correctly follows the steps that he had learned in the workshop, I just acknowledge the good approach and don't say much.

This example of pairing with George often happens after a workshop or when you are teaching a programmer something new. It's a good approach to use to help you solidify the acquired knowledge in the production code of a team. This is because it often happens that a classroom code base is easy to tackle, but the production code base is another beast. George is a lot more confident about applying the new technique after a couple of 2-hour sessions of pairing with me, using the Beginner-Advanced technique.

Remarks

This technique is different from the Pairing-Trainee technique. Here, we talk about teaching a junior programmer how to code, while Pairing-Trainee is about teaching programmers of any level how to use pair programming.

The Beginner-Beginner technique

This is a technique when you put two junior programmers, or beginners, together to pair with each other.

Setup

Typically, the setup for this technique is two people at a computer with just one keyboard and a mouse.

Rotation

Rotations are not as often as you would expect with experienced programmers – perhaps every 10 or 20 minutes.

Advantages

I don't see many advantages to this technique. Instead of letting one experienced programmer struggle, you have a pair of people struggling. And struggling together means that they might, maybe, get something done.

Disadvantages

There are many disadvantages to this technique:

- First of all, the two partners won't be able to learn that much. They will struggle a lot with not much result.

- The two partners will struggle a lot in an attempt to produce something, which is frustrating. Additionally, if it's their first working experience, they are likely to remember it for the rest of their lives.

- Struggling could lead to a lot of negative opinions about the methods that the two partners are using. In fact, they might even consider pairing as a negative thing from the onset and, by extension, the code base they are trying to get, the IDE, or any tool that is connected to this experience.

I wouldn't like to have a first-time learning experience like this, and I hope you wouldn't want that either!

When to use it

Please don't use this technique; it's more of an anti-pattern.

I was invited to an organization to evaluate their overall technical management, tools, and practices. During these gigs, I spend most of the time talking to as many people as I can and taking time to observe the workspace of the teams. Here, I noticed that one team had more junior programmers who had been hired only recently. Instead of having a formal and informal induction from more experienced programmers, the junior programmers were left to learn by themselves. As they were not enough computers at that point, two programmers shared the same computer and tried to get their heads around the code base. After seeing this, I asked them to have a chat. They said that everything seemed to be really confusing, and they already weren't enjoying working there. This is how counterproductive Beginner-Beginner pairing can be. After one year, all the junior programmers left the organization. It's no wonder, considering how they were treated by the hiring organization during their first few weeks.

Remarks

I wouldn't recommend using this technique.

The Ping-Pong technique

Beginning with from Driver-Navigator, we have two roles that change relatively often. The driver is always in charge, and the navigator can suggest ideas. But the two roles change quite often.

Setup

For this technique, you will need a setup for two people: two keyboards, two mice, and ideally two monitors that are connected to the same computer with a mirrored screen.

Rotation

There are several ways in which to rotate with this technique, and they are explained as follows:

- **Timeboxing**: Using a timer, the partners change when the timer rings. The usual time slots are between 5 and 10 minutes. The condition is that when you pass the keyboard, the code works and you have finished your current idea.

- **Test-Driven Development** (**TDD**): In TDD, you follow the Red, Green, Refactor cycle. With Ping-Pong, one person always writes a test, and the other person implements the test and refactors it. Then, the second person writes a test and gives the first person the opportunity to implement and refactor it. It's Ping-Pong because you always pass the test around to your partner, in the same way that you would hit the Ping-Pong ball to go to the other side of the table.

- **Task bases**: The pair splits the work into small tasks of no more than 30 minutes each. Then, each partner gets to be a driver or a navigator, one after the other. This technique works really well because you can see real progress, and it's comforting to cross tasks off a list and say they're done. However, it can be difficult if you are not used to splitting tasks into such small increments. Anyway, practicing to split tasks in small increments is a good lesson, as a by-product of the technique itself.

Advantages

As both partners can write code for an equal amount of time, on average, this technique tends to be more effective and can even generate better results more quickly.

The fact that the partners switch more often forces them to take smaller steps. This means that you cannot start a complex change for 3 or 4 hours, which will most likely get you stuck. From this point of view, it's an advantage that the partners learn how to decompose a bigger 3 or 4-hour step into smaller 5 or 10-minute steps that allow them to create a flow. You can minimize the time lost from getting stuck and trying to fix things.

This can be a very useful method to learn TDD, as it forces you to think about how the code evolves in small iterations. This pairing technique helps to set a discipline to the Red-Green-Refactor cycle, and it's a good addition to TDD.

Disadvantages

Because of the frequent rotations, this technique can lead to context switching and the partners becoming tired more quickly.

Additionally, when the partners don't agree on what path to take with their solution, the code can get repetitive, and not much gets done. It's a learning process for both partners, usually a much-needed learning process, but it can still be ineffective and frustrating.

When to use it

This is a good technique for more experienced pair programmers. Usually, after a few weeks of using the Driver-Navigator technique, I would introduce the Ping-Pong technique for a while to see what the team thinks.

When using TDD, Ping-Pong is my go-to pair programming approach. Once, I was pairing with a few advanced programmers, who wanted to boost their TDD practices. Naturally, I asked them to use Ping-Pong. Our sessions were fun, energetic, slightly tiring, but very fulfilling for all of us. We saw progress and could also bounce ideas while changing the roles in our pair. At the end of the session, which took around 2 hours all in all with some breaks, we finished with a debrief. The main comments that were made during our debrief were that it was intensive learning, we didn't know how the time passed so quickly, and working like this really made sense.

Remarks

This is an interesting approach that can lead to a relatively intellectually intense activity of trying to write a good test, with an equally good next step. It allows both partners the opportunity to look at the short term and the long term, and it creates the premise for good software design.

Summary

So far, we have discussed pair programming techniques, where they are useful, and how they can be used, along with nuances for each technique. The Driver-Navigator technique is a classic approach to pair programming, while the Pairing-Trainee method helps programmers learn how to use pairing. The Beginner-Advanced technique is a method of teaching a new topic by using pair programming. The Beginner-Beginner technique is an approach that I don't recommend, and Ping-Pong pair programming is especially useful with TDD. Try using these techniques in the appropriate context. And what better way to understand these techniques than to experiment with all of them, practice them, and then decide on the right method to use yourself. However, don't do that just yet! Let's examine how we can improve the preceding techniques with pair programming styles.

Improving pair programming with styles

A **pair programming style** is a specific way to behave while pairing. It is an addition to the techniques that we discussed earlier. Remember that not all of these styles are compatible with all the techniques that we mentioned. Choosing the right style for the right context can boost any pair programming session.

Consider the following working styles: when working in a pair, your style could be to let your partner to work as they like or say only a few clear, direct comments. Alternatively, your style might be to guide everyone during every moment of the process. I have even heard people who choose the style of not interfering and taking every chance to explain something new to their partners at the right moment, mostly when the code is in a stable state.

So, a style is a mix of how involved you are, how much space you give to your partner, how much you step up, but also how you communicate. Let's explore each of these styles in more detail and find out when is best to use them.

Unplanned pairing

This is the most common type of pairing for when you are stuck, you need some advice, or you want some expertise from a colleague. Typically, you ask if they can help, and you sit at the same desk with the problem in your head and start talking through it. In this scenario, you don't have clear roles; rather, the focus is to solve the particular problem that was raised.

Many programmers don't know that this is pairing. Instead, they think of it as asking for advice.

Pros

Unplanned pairing comes naturally; there are no specific rules to take into account. It's easy to set up and not much overhead is required.

Cons

This style is not necessarily the most effective way of pairing. Usually, it just involves a few team members who start working with each other.

The pairing approaches of different people might diverge from the most efficient method. It's very difficult to see what needs to be improved when you are paired with people who do the same work as what you do.

When to use it

This technique, probably, works best in its natural form rather than not happening at all. It's not ideal; however, it's a start, and it gets people used to the idea of working in a pair as opposed to working solo.

When people start unplanned pairing and like it, it's just a matter of discovering a better pairing style and they learn it at once. However, when people have used unplanned pairing and have felt awful, been criticized, or been mocked, then it's going to be a lot more difficult to make them want to pair again, even if they are doing so in a different context.

Traditional pairing

Traditional pairing occurs when you have two partners in front of the computer and they work without much thought about anything else. Typically, people pair with colleagues they like to pair with, and they tend to stick to one another.

This is a form of planned pairing, the simplest one, and it works when one pair says, "I want to pair on this topic because we will go faster," or something such as "You know this topic better, so I would like to pair with you in order to learn it as well."

You might have one person typing for days and the other just observing. Or, you might have a rotation in the pair. It varies depending on the people involved and how they feel at that particular moment.

When you are focused on getting things done, the more experienced person will take the lead, and the other will just follow for long periods of time. This is a good approach as the more experienced can work at a faster pace and will depend on the partner to point out any syntax mistakes or small errors when needed. In this way, the observer can learn how to get things done in that part of the code base, or with that tool, or learn more about that part of the domain logic.

When you focus on learning, the experience can vary depending upon the fact that you can be a programmer or not. Nevertheless, the focus, in this case, is on learning and not on getting things done. You don't always have that clear focus, as you might divert your attention from the end goal in order to show some details of the tool or of the system that you are teaching or learning.

Most of the time, one of the partners will decide to take the lead in the pair and make most of the decisions. Usually, the more experienced, more senior, or more outspoken partner will take this role. While this can be a good thing, as soon as communication becomes just a one-way street and their partner is constantly at loggerheads with them and not getting through, it starts becoming a problem.

The quality of communication depends on the two programmers involved. Sometimes, it can get tricky with arguments or fights on how to do a certain thing. However, it can also be a smooth process and flow without any incidents. Typically, for untrained traditional pairings, there is very little understanding about how to communicate properly and, additionally, how important communication is when doing pair programming.

Compared to other styles of pairing, traditional pairing is quieter. The driver leads the way, sometimes explaining things, but there isn't much debate or discussion.

Pros

It's good to pair up, get things done, or learn with this style because you will do these things more quickly in a pair than if you were working in isolation. Traditional pairing is a good approach when you need to learn a new business domain, a library, or a new tool or technique.

If we consider the point of view between the learning quantity and quality, it might be the most effective method of pairing.

Cons

As each person might do what they feel is necessary, without much experience of pair programming, they might make wrong decisions that create tension in the pair.

Quite often, the leading partner can make decisions without explaining them too much or too well, and this can generate tension or frustration for the other person.

Traditional pairing is not the most effective way of pairing, and it is mainly judged by the coding outcome.

When using traditional pairing remotely, it is difficult to stay engaged. Since the navigator doesn't have a very active role, they can easily be distracted, or even lose focus while the driver is focused on getting something done. To overcome this shortcoming, the driver needs to always explain what they are doing in greater detail and often ask for feedback from the navigator. Additionally, the driver needs to try to include the navigator in the conversation in order to heat up the pairing activity.

Best suited for

Beginners in pair programming benefit from trying this style. It's easier to approach. Not a lot of social and communication skills are needed to use this style as compared to the other pair programming styles.

Elastic pairing

Elastic pairing is a situation when any pair can take the keyboard and continue.

This is a pairing style where decisions are made with the consensus of the two partners. The two partners know how to communicate, can briefly explain their points of view, and accept the other's argument. The partners try to find the best solution for the problem at hand rather than trying to impose their opinion based on ego.

There is a good rule with elastic pair programming: when someone is watching you, you need to work at a slower pace. Quite often, you need to slow down, and if you go any faster, you are likely to make mistakes. For beginners to pairing, slowing down might feel like you are being less effective. However, to people who are advanced in pair programming, slowing down feels like the right thing to do. When you slow down, it's less likely that you will break things, get stuck, or make mistakes. Additionally, you can start to build up a state of flow, which you can keep at that pace for long periods of time.

This style feels very natural; It's similar to two old friends talking to each other and never wanting to stop. Because of that, it often leads to a good flow, good progress, and a higher quality of product. When you are pairing, you might think only one hour has passed, then look at the clock and find that many hours have passed, which means you were, or still are, in a state of flow.

Elastic pairing means that you stop implementing the traditional driver and navigator roles. Each partner can be more upfront or at the back of the programming stage, depending on the context. The two partners behave without formal roles, drivers or navigators, and without any of the two partners getting annoyed.

With elastic pairing, you will often ask your partner for feedback and whether they want to continue being the driver. There are even moments when both partners are driving – each one of the two partners writing very small batches of code, such as a few words or letters.

So, elastic pairing feels as though you are working with someone whom you have known for a long time, and you can complete each other's words, sentences, and expressions.

For me, this is the best expression of collaboration between equal peers. It allows you to work together with respect for the other's point of view, care, and empathy for what the other person thinks. It involves a mix of technical traits, communication, and social types of behaviors, which generate a very productive and almost ideal working environment.

When using elastic pair programming, it's helpful to set up rules such as no phones, no distractions, and to remain involved even if you are not writing code.

Pros

This style is one of the most productive ways of working for experienced and senior programmers who are open to pairing with anyone from their team.

When working in this way, that is, with elastic pair programming, work becomes fun. And with great enjoyment usually also comes great productivity. The satisfaction of getting things done also generates high-quality products and reduces any tensions within the team or pressures from outside the team to get things done within a particular timeframe.

Elastic pair programming feels more engaging for each partner. There isn't any point where you will get bored or feel that you are being left out. You are required to be there, with a focus of 100%, and if you aren't, your pair will feel it immediately.

Cons

You need many skills, mostly non-technical, to be able to achieve such a balanced method of pair programming. Far too often, programmers are only taught technical skills in organizations; however, social and communication skills are not considered to be that important. This is a management mistake that can affect the whole organization and prevent the efficient implementation of approaches such as pair programming to their full extent.

It is debatable whether you can only have a few people in a team using this approach. Usually, a few people who really like each other become friends and start working together. This situation might be problematic, as you don't want to have islands of boosted productivity, based on self-selecting groups, and the rest are left to do the best they can, just because they don't fit into that group.

Elastic pairing is not useful in certain situations, for example, if you want to learn about the business domain or when you are pairing with people at different levels of seniority. Traditional pairing will help you to learn more about the domain and the technologies that you are focusing on.

If you haven't used elastic pair programming before, it is more difficult to use it remotely. It can be especially difficult to enforce the no-distraction rules (for example, no phones, chats, or email) we spoke about.

When to use it

This is best suited for experienced programmers, who have paired for a while and greatly appreciate each other's opinions at any given time.

Strong-style pairing

Strong-style pairing is very different from the other styles we have mentioned so far, and, sometimes, it is the opposite of other pair programming styles. In this pairing style, we have the driver who writes the code and focuses on the small details, in the short term, but cannot decide anything. Then, we have the navigator who makes all the decisions, focusing on long-term decisions. We sometimes say that the driver is a smart keyboard, who is only doing something when they are told to. The only reason why the driver focuses on the smaller details is to do what the navigator has in mind while doing it.

Sometimes, you might find that the two don't understand where they are going. At that point, when something is unclear, the two need to stop working and have a dialogue about what they need to do next.

Similar to traditional-style pairing, both the driver and the navigator have the same focus, to try to solve the problem as fast as they can with the highest quality possible.

This is the most difficult style of pairing, especially for the navigator who is taking many responsibilities on their head. You can think of this as though we are forming a pair programming body where the navigator is the brain, and the driver is the hands that touch the keyboard. The reason behind this is that in order for an idea to become functional, it needs to first pass through someone else's brain.

It's not always the case that an experienced navigator knows what to do next. Sometimes, the navigator will try things and develop the code in certain directions just to see where it goes. It's usual to do that when you are solo programming. However, in this situation, the driver might feel that the navigator doesn't know what they are doing. That is why the navigator needs to ask the driver for some trust, particularly in the short term, while trying things that might seem weird. You need to do that as a navigator because when your pair doesn't trust you, it's difficult to explain, in logical terms, something you cannot yet grasp to its full extent. That is why the navigator experiments with different things, in order to better understand a certain detail of the potential code.

The navigator needs to possess extremely good communication skills. It's not just about what to say, but also how to say it, and when to say it. Additionally, it's about the chain of different small communications that add up and make things clear to the driver in terms of what to do next.

One of the most important guidelines to succeed with Strong-Style pairing is that the navigator needs to communicate gradually, from generic to more specific details.

A guideline for communicating to the driver is to use three steps, as follows:

1. **Intention**:

   First of all, the navigator needs to express their intention. This needs to be something generic, yet clear. For example, "*I would like to implement an A* search algorithm for this list,*" or "*We need to use a strategy pattern for these cases.*"

2. **Location**:

   After that, mention the location. You could say, "Line 34," or "Line 34 and a half," if you want the driver to insert a new line after line 34. If you need to create a new file, say something such as "Search namespace, algorithms folder."

3. **Details**:

   Then, only at the end, after expressing your intention and the location, the navigator should delve into the details. The details can be more or less, depending on the driver. Sometimes, it's enough to simply say, "Please implement this interface and all the methods from it for class X." However, if your driver is a novice, then you need to go into more detail by saying, "Create a new class, implement the interface to the new class, generate all the methods from the interface with the help of the IDE, implement first the `doThis` method, then the `doThat` method, making sure you respect the contract of the interface."

Very often, I see the second approach being used when it isn't needed, and the driver already knows what they need to do. This is a waste of time, but it can also be frustrating for the driver, as they might feel like they are less useful than a smart keyboard.

Communication becomes easier to manage once you use these three steps. Remember, it's not something that you do naturally, and it needs practice and perseverance from the navigator. Additionally, it brings a lot of clarity and flow, and it reduces any friction caused by the driver being unclear on what to do next.

The driver is a smart keyboard, as mentioned earlier. This means the driver needs to ask for clarification when needed, but they cannot make any decision on their own. Communicating well is as important for the driver as it is for the navigator.

All the decisions come from the navigator. It's an interesting feeling being the driver, as you focus solely on writing the code, and you need to empty your mind of the larger-scale decisions. For some, it's great fun to pair like that, while for others, it feels like they are neglecting their capabilities on purpose. And that's not necessarily a bad thing, to focus with less bandwidth, less brainpower, and just do some simpler and smaller activities.

The partners can choose to rotate with each other more or less often in Strong-Style pairing. You can use the timeboxing technique or rotate after bigger independent chunks of code start working, and you can pass the navigator's role with a clean slate to the driver.

Rotation comes with more context switching compared to the other pair programming styles. The driver needs to remove themselves from the simpler, more comfortable role of a smart keyboard and into a deeply involved strategist and designer role as the navigator.

Pros

This pair programming style is very useful for knowledge transfer. It's mainly used by technical coaches, team leaders, or very experienced senior programmers.

When using Strong-Style pairing, the navigator is far more engaged than in other pair programming styles. Since the navigator becomes the front figure of the experience, they need to be very present and active.

Cons

If done wrong, this style generates a lot of frustration. And the partners that have experienced it, even in the wrong way, might never want to come back to it, even if after a while.

Using this style excessively, that is, on a regular basis for many weeks, might make the style less effective. This is because the people who were involved have started to understand more about the basics of what the partners were doing. So, switching to a different style where the partners are more equal, or having rotations of between 5 and 15 minutes with Strong-Style pairing, would be a lot more beneficial.

When to use it

Strong-Style pairing is suited for any programmer in the driver's seat. However, for the navigator, a very experienced programmer, team leader, or technical coach is needed. You can definitely try Strong-Style pairing without a very experienced navigator, but there's a big risk that things will derail fast, and many would consider that this way of working doesn't make much sense.

Strong-Style pairing is useful when people are very used to their code but don't know how to refactor it. In this situation, it is very useful to use Strong-Style pairing because the driver would know how to navigate around the code, but they won't know how to refactor it or use a specific coding technique.

Once, I was at a client site and was pairing, for the first time, with an experienced programmer. I was pairing with the kind of programmer who would prefer not to give the keyboard away. In this situation, Strong-Style pairing was preferable, as I saw that he was very attached to his tools, keyboard, and mouse. I started working with him, being just a shadow, and asking simple clarification questions when I was not clear as to what he was doing. Little by little, I started having opinions about what we could do better. Through small steps, I started taking control of the development direction, simply by suggesting ideas and discussing them with my partner. I swiftly became the strong partner and started helping my partner without touching the keyboard for even a moment.

Summary

Pair programming styles make a key difference to both a programmer who uses pairing and also a well-versed programmer who can use pair programming effectively in a variety of places and contexts. Constantly adapting to your partner is one of the essential characteristics of an experienced pair programmer, and pair programming styles occupy an important role in that. After spicing the pair programming techniques with styles, we can now look at how to organize ourselves for pair programming.

Organizing pair programming

An organization can think about implementing pair programming in many different ways. Naturally, people who are friends, or work well together, will pair with each other. Additionally, people who are outspoken, or extroverts, will find each other and start pairing up. But what do we do with the rest? Maybe there are individuals who want to pair-program in the organization, but they are afraid to start, or they are embarrassed to pair with that programmer who is very good and thinks they are too good for them. Imposter syndrome happens everywhere in knowledge-based work environments and affects any knowledge worker, and programmers are no exception.

So, we need to do something about this situation in order to generalize pair programming in the organization. In the following sections, we discuss a number of commonly used options to generalize the use of pair programming in any organization.

Round-robin pairing

Round-robin pairing is where every team member partners with every other team member, in a clear order.

First, we create a list of tasks, and the first pair then picks the first task and this continues with the following pairs and tasks until the list ends. For the next set of tasks, you change partners, making sure that none of the original partners are the same. It continues like this until you return back to the initial partner structure. There are no individual tasks; there are just team tasks that get (self)assigned to partners. Of course, you might want to make sure that the tasks are (self)assigned in a way that the pair can solve the tasks, in a timely manner. Sometimes, we have specialists in some areas, or we have people who have never touched that area of the code.

This way of organizing pair programming is effective, transparent, clear, and easy to use. However, bear in mind that it won't please everyone. You might start having conflicts because *Jane doesn't want to pair with Julia*. Or that *John would like to pair more often with Jane*. For some teams, in some contexts, round-robin pairing can feel forced, even coerced. Because of that, it is important to get the approval of the whole team before you start using it. It's OK to use it one or two times as a pairing experiment, but then you need to make a short retrospective and ask the team whether they like the method and whether they would like to continue with it.

Promiscuous pairing

Promiscuous pairing can be described as an unselective approach in which you use an indiscriminate manner to find partners within the team. Promiscuous pairing means that we want everyone to pair with each other and to switch partners as quickly as possible. It's not as strict as round-robin pairing, but someone will oversee the process so that you don't have selective pairing or just parts of the team are promiscuous.

This is another method of spreading information and practices around the team. With these rapid changes, the partners will receive the same information more quickly than they would with other approaches to organized pair programming. The partners change relatively often, and you can pair with a few people daily, even on tasks that another pair has already started beforehand. In comparison to round-robin paring, here, you would pair instead in timeboxes, but that's not necessarily a rule. If you have very small tasks that can be done in one or two hours, then you can use promiscuous pairing without needing to continue another pair's task.

Promiscuous pairing is sometimes difficult to accept. It might sound crazy to change partners every couple of hours, and it can feel unstable and unreliable, among other things that generate instability. Additionally, as with any situation, people might feel forced to pair with someone they don't like to work with. This latter situation can definitely cause tensions. Nevertheless, it's important to learn from everyone, and any team leader or senior programmer in the team should try and encourage any colleagues to be open-minded about the pairing. Any personal situations of incompatibility need to be resolved by taking into account each specific context, considering the current situation and the history of the pair. There can be many reasons, historical or personal, that generate this current incompatibility. Some of them can be resolved, while others are very difficult to solve.

Selective pairing

You can describe **selective pairing** as pairing with your friends and neighbors and ignoring the rest. This is the natural way to start pairing. This is of course, applicable where anyone would choose someone who is open to working like this. Even if you wish to convince your colleagues, some of them won't want to work in a pair. So, in the end, you have a self-selecting group of people who will work by using pair programming.

This is a very good first step toward pair programming. However, leaving out a part of the team is not a good idea, at least in the long term. You will end up with two teams in one, that start diverging their practices, beliefs, tools, and more. After working like that for a while, you will need to see whether all the team members want to pair, at least on some type of tasks, or whether it's a better idea to split the team into two: a team that uses pair programming, and a team that doesn't use pair programming.

We need to acknowledge that pair programming is not for everyone, at least in the beginning. Some people, the early adopters, want to take a chance with this new idea. Howver, there is also an early majority that might be formed, if the early adopters create compelling arguments. Then, you might convince the remaining workers to start using pair programming. It can take weeks or months. And in the end, you still have laggards who don't want to pair. And that's fine. Pair programming isn't necessarily for everyone. We don't need to force this practice but show how it works for us, and invite people to try it for themselves.

Many teams keep using this approach for years. And even if it's suboptimal, it's still better than no pairing at all.

We have discussed a few typical situations of how to organize pair programming within an organization. We didn't go into too much detail, as it's not the main purpose of this book. However, I highly encourage you to learn more and ask for help from a technical coach when organizing pair programming for the first time. The saying, *"The devil is in the details,"* is very appropriate to the task of organizing pair programming, and even an experienced technical coach can make mistakes when dealing with a new team. After we have organized ourselves, the next question arises: *How often do we need to pair?* Let's review some answers in the next section.

How often do we need to pair?

This is a very common question that gets asked when using pair programming for the first time. The answer to this is very difficult since it depends heavily on the context of the organization, team, product, code, features, time available, and many other aspects. Let's answer some of the more common scenarios.

Should you pair for the whole day?

Especially at the beginning, pair programming can be extremely tiring. This is because we are doing activities that we aren't used to doing such as explaining every step, thinking about options, trying to explain alternative options, and more. Additionally, besides being tiring, pair programming is also very intensive. Due to these factors, I wouldn't recommend pairing for more than 1 or 2 hours per day, to begin with.

Once when you have paired for a while, and you have adjusted to how tiring it can be, you can pair for more than 1 or 2 hours per day. Maybe you can try pairing for half of the day. When you become a regular pair programmer, it's natural for you to want to pair always. However, not all tasks benefit from the increased efficiency caused by pair programming. So, we must choose pairing for those tasks that involve a higher complexity of understanding, where there is a greater probability for mistakes, where there is a greater capacity for analysis, where there is high impact, and more. You can solo program the remaining tasks that are basic and where there isn't much complexity to tackle. In such situations, you would just waste the other person's time.

Should you pair daily?

I would recommend beginners to pair every couple of days. In this way, they can get used to the new practice and begin understanding the small important details of pair programming. Pairing, let's say, once every month won't bring much benefit, as you will have already forgotten what you had learned after a break of one month between the two pair programming sessions. So, that is why, for beginners, a good choice is to pair for a couple of hours every couple of days.

For regular and advanced pair programmers, how often they pair depends on their list of tasks, their product, and more. I would recommend them to pair as much they can, as long as it makes sense from a productivity point of view. However, you should also take breaks from pairing, for instance, only pairing three days out of five.

Should you pair weekly?

For a beginner, pairing weekly is not often enough. However, it's better than nothing. The problem with pairing so rarely is that it's difficult to learn how to pair well. And by the time you get to the next session, your memory of the previous session is already fuzzy. So, you need less time between the sessions in order to make it efficient and easier for you.

For regular and advanced programmers, pairing weekly, if possible, can work well. I have had periods when I was pairing a lot less because of the different projects that I had. And those projects wouldn't benefit from pair programming. So, it's fine to not pair that often, as long as you have learned and understood what pairing is and how it can help you.

Working solo versus working in a pair

Working solo has many benefits, and just because we are discussing pair programming, we don't need to minimize solo programming.

It's good to solo program when pairing doesn't bring any noticeable benefit. For example, when there is not much learning or knowledge transfer, you are working on trivial tasks, have only simple problems to solve, and more. Additionally, solo programming is easier for introverts, as they lose so much energy when pairing or being in a group.

Pairing with another person comes with the clear advantage of interactivity, learning, knowledge sharing, tackling difficult tasks easily, and even creating a lot of fun for many people.

In my head, there's no one versus the other argument but how I can effectively use each of them. My advice is to not pair day in and day out, but also not to solo program without any interaction. Both are useful methods of working for everybody, but the dosage depends on each of us. Try pairing, and find the right dose for you.

You need to decide how much you need to pair yourself, as situations may differ and there is no generic answer. Your skills, your colleague's willingness to pair, the way your organization works, the project you are working in, and the technologies you are using are just a few of the factors that will affect how much you need to pair. In any situation, it's better to try it regularly, at longer intervals, than not trying it at all.

After observing thousands of pairs working during Coderetreats, hands-on workshops, or when consulting with different organizations, I think that the first essential skill you need to have for pair programming is to communicate well. That is why, in the following section, we will explore the different communication methods you can use.

Exploring different communication methods

OK, this is pure psychology, but when we work in a team, we need to communicate well in order to achieve our common team goals. Often, I consider communication one of the most important aspects of working together. Even particular, specific, and rare skills aren't as important as good communication.

Being professional means that you can have work relations with anyone who behaves decently and be able to give feedback to and receive feedback from anyone. The same happens in a pair or in a team.

When programming in a pair, it's not the time to show our ego, brag, shame others with our knowledge, or put pressure on our partners. It is quite the opposite: it's the time to explain, wait for the information to be absorbed, explain again, and then explain again. Be patient and guide your partner in order to make them understand your point of view. This is important. I have seen so many pair programming sessions fail simply because the partners were too aggressive with one another and didn't listen to each other. Sometimes, they wanted to do the same thing, but they communicated so badly that they couldn't understand that they both wanted to achieve the same common purpose.

I am by no means an expert in psychology or communication; however, working with teams has led me to learn more and more about these topics, and I will tell you how I approach three main communication behaviors inside a team next.

Aggressive communication

Aggressive communication means that we focus on our own needs, preferences, or feelings over the needs of the people around us. Aggressiveness generates more aggressiveness. It's never a good idea to respond to aggressive communication with more aggression.

When you find yourself in an aggressive stance, try to focus on the facts and how you can reach a common ground.

Submissive communication

Submissive communication means that we focus on other people's needs at our personal expense. This way of communicating will create internal frustration, and it will make us undervalue our own goals and contributions. When you find yourself in a submissive stance, try to think about how your ideas bring value to the current conversation. State your point of view, and open your heart to others.

Assertive communication

Assertive communication sits between the other two ways of communicating that we have just mentioned. Here, you focus on your personal needs but take into account and consider the needs, preferences, and feelings of other people around you. Communicating like that feels warm and thoughtful to others.

When using assertive communication, we focus on the facts and convey our purpose and willingness to find a common ground.

Making a difference with the right words, tone, and clarity

Continuing with the topic of communication, most of the time, when two people pair with each other in a nice and productive manner, they are able to communicate well with each other.

That is why we need to approach our colleagues by using appropriate words. The words that we use have meaning, and it's important to acknowledge those meanings. Sometimes, we use words that in themselves have complex definitions. Saying *"I would like to build a strategy for algorithms to decouple this low cohesion structure"* shows that there is a lot of knowledge being transmitted. If your pair doesn't know the meaning of all those words, then don't use them. Instead, spend your time explaining, in detail, what you mean. Ask your partner, each time, whether they understand what you mean when you use complex words in a sentence, for example, *strategy*, *cohesion*, *stub*, *mock*, *double*, and more.

The tone that we use is a second communication channel alongside the words that we use. Because of that, our tone needs to be in agreement with the words we use. We might be in uncomfortable situations when pairing. I know I am almost always put in novel situations, with technologies I don't know so well and with partners that I don't know that much. Because of them, we might feel overwhelmed, stressed, or tired. All of these emotions are reflected in our tone.

From time to time, I recommend that you try and actively listen to your tone. Ask yourself the following questions:

- *Is my tone in conjunction with the words am I using?*
- *Does my tone seem aggressive?*
- *How can I make my tone more appropriate to the context?*

I know it's not easy to do that, and it requires a lot of practice. Moreover, it requires you to ask for a lot of feedback from your partners, colleagues, friends, and family. It can be extremely difficult to change the way you communicate through your tone of voice. My only advice here is to ask for feedback, listen to the feedback you receive, and try to improve yourself.

There is that saying by Albert Einstein that *"If you can't explain it simply, you don't understand it well enough."* When we pair, we need to explain a lot; most of time, when we pair, we either explain what we write, explain what we think we should do next, or discuss the impact of our decisions on the future. However you put it, you need to have a continuous flow of explanation – one that is almost as long as the pairing session itself. That is why I recommend that you try the following steps whenever you explain something to your partner:

1. Prepare before explaining your point of view.
2. Take the time to explain, and don't rush.
3. Ask for feedback at the end of your explanation: *Was I clear, and do you have any questions?*
4. If your explanation is longer than 5 minutes, ask for feedback every 5 minutes or so to check whether you need to come back to some explanations or whether you can go on.

We have only scratched the surface of the topic of communication methods. Improving communication is a lifelong learning experience; we always have something new to learn about ourselves and others. Calmness, brevity, good vocabulary usage, and adopting the appropriate tone sounds easy; however, once you ask for feedback from people, you will see that it's a lot more difficult than it seems. So, the best approach is to consider yourself a constant student with continual openness for feedback from your peers.

Pair programming best practices

In this section, we'll look at some of the best practices to use when doing pair programming. Most of the best practices discussed here are not related to programming but to communication and social interactions. Sometimes, when I dive into this topic, I am told that this is *common sense*, but bear in mind that my common sense can be different from your common sense, and radically different from someone else's common sense.

These are guidelines that we need to use. And depending on each person's experience and background, some are part of their usual behavior, while some aren't. All of this behavior is either taught or self-taught, and we always have a bit more to learn and polish in order to improve ourselves.

Taking notes while pair programming

You can use a notebook, index cards, sticky notes, a piece of paper, a tablet, or even a second computer to take notes. It's important not to break the current flow when you observe something that needs to be repaired, or improved, or just something interesting that you would like to highlight.

Typically, the navigator takes notes because the driver is busy with the small details, and it would be more difficult for them to take notes. However, with experienced pair programmers, you will often have a situation where both partners will take notes.

After a while, the two partners need to start discussing their notes – including each item – and then deciding what to do next. It's important to do this every 1 or 2 hours at least, if not more often. It depends, of course, on the current course of action, and stopping in the middle of something to discuss your notes is not a good option.

Note-taking is also important because it fixes some ideas or concepts in your head. It's a proven fact that writing something down will make you remember it more easily, sooner, and more quickly. So, particularly when you are learning something new in pair programming, a notebook should be a not-to-miss item in front of you.

Starting with some small talk

Usually, I like starting with a small chat to ask my partner how they are, how they feel, what they have done so far, and more. It's always a good idea to start with some small talk for a few minutes in order to smoothly transition into the serious order of business that will follow.

During these minutes, you might find about your partner's disposition. In this way, you discover whether it's a good idea to be more incisive or more relaxed and whether it's a good idea to take on difficult tasks or simpler tasks.

Small talk is very different in various cultures, so use it as you see fit in your culture. Nevertheless, I have found it useful to use small talk to get a head start in any culture; it's just that the details and the duration were different.

Emptying your cup

In order to be able to learn something new, you need to have the openness to realize that you don't know everything. It becomes difficult, especially for senior programmers, to understand that they can learn many things even from junior programmers. Learning is our job as knowledge workers, and we need to learn from *anyone* who can teach something useful to us.

There is a story that comes from an ancient Asian tale about a student who was reluctant to learn and a master who explained how important openness is:

[..] Finally, the master poured a full serving of tea into his own cup, and into the cup of the student. Then he told the student he wanted to give to him some of the tea from his own cup. He began pouring tea from his cup into the student's cup, but the student's cup was already full, and all the tea from the master's cup spilled out over the cup onto the surface below.

The student said, "Master, you can't pour anything into my cup until I empty it to make room for what you are trying to give me." And the master replied, "Yes I know. And I can't give you any new thoughts or ideas or perspectives on life's lessons until you clear out some thoughts that are already teeming in your mind to make room for what I have to teach you." Then the master paused for a brief moment, meeting the student's eyes with his own knowing look and calmly but sternly said: " If you truly seek understanding, then first, empty your cup!"

So, if you want to use pair programming to its full efficiency, I recommend you, first, empty your cup, and then start pairing.

Debriefing

Perhaps it comes as a cliché, but we do need to talk about feedback.

Feedback is very important when working collaboratively in a team. It's even more important when pair programming. In this scenario, you are working very closely with someone, and it's a good opportunity to praise their good knowledge and behavior and, at the same time, to come with improvement suggestions for their flaws.

The best approach is to create a moment of openness for the pair, usually at the end of the pair programming session, where you debrief them about what happened. Each of the programmers will think about the following:

- What I liked about this session
- What I would improve

You get to discuss each one of the items presented by your pair. Then, after this debrief, it's a good idea to make a list of future actions. These can be very small actions such as starting earlier or using a different chair. Alternatively, they can be more substantial actions such as explaining more when driving, making a few design diagrams on paper before coding, and more.

Don't get personal; try to think about situations and approaches to that particular situation. Try to understand whether the approaches of both persons from the pair were appropriate, given the context.

Be careful not to fall into the blame game, believing that only the other person was responsible for any mishaps during your pairing session. You were there too, and you were both in that situation together.

Another very important note is that feedback is given for the future, and there is no need to blame someone by looking at the past. You cannot change the past, but we all can learn from it. So, consider finding lessons that you learned in the past for the future.

Dialogue courtesy

In a good conversation, listening is more important than speaking. Listening actively to what your pair is saying is very important for efficient collaboration. If you feel something is unclear, ask clarification questions such as *"What do you mean by that?"*, *"Could you please elaborate on this topic?"*, *"I'm sorry, but I didn't understand why we need to do this,"* or *"Could we discuss this some more?"* After a series of clarification questions, you will feel as though you know a lot more about what your partner is saying, and it's a good moment to form an opinion. Far too often, I see opinions arising before clarifying a topic. And then we stop having a dialogue, and we start having a pointlessly heated discussion.

Before starting to speak, try to think about what you are going to say and how to express your thoughts. Sometimes, I take notes on a piece of paper with the main points I want to express. I try to think about how to frame my thoughts. Only after that, I wait for a good moment to broach the subject. After expressing my point of view, I ask my partner, *"Was I clear enough?"* or *"Do you have any questions?"*

Having this dialogue courtesy helps a lot to clarify topics, and it decreases the probability of starting a sterile argument. It's a good practice in almost all collaboration contexts within a team.

Building confidence – committing often and having good unit tests

When writing a big chunk of code at once, our brain cannot process all the information that we put in there, and things start becoming fuzzy. This is a great opportunity for a mistake to sneak in. We can cheat our brains by taking smaller steps because when we finish a small part and commit it, our brains relax and put that information into a drawer.

That's why there's the question, *"How often should we commit?"* My answer is as often as you can. I tend to commit locally in systems such as Git or Mercurial once every 5 to 15 minutes. Once you are able to commit often, you can really get into a flow. You will feel less tired and more aware of your progress.

Unit tests are among the fastest mode of quality feedback cycle for you. Use it as much as possible, and run your tests as often as possible. One unit test should run between 1 and 10 milliseconds. That means you should be able to run between 100 and, 1000 unit tests and not get bored while waiting. You can also have tens of thousands or millions of unit tests, but then you need to group them on modules, and then run only the unit tests that affect the module that you are working on.

Having unit tests and committing often is a great opportunity for a special type of dialogue for a pair. You can come up with an atomic item of work (which are a lot smaller than ordinary tasks) together with your pair, write tests for it, commit it, and then see how you made 1% progress.

Trusting your pair

You know that trust is easy to lose and hard to win. This is also true for pair programming. However, start by trusting your partner and then focus on improving anything with feedback.

Trust is very important when we pair. Far too often, programmers join a session full of suspicion and are waiting for a small thing to go wrong, just so that they can say that it doesn't work. Start by having some trust, then try pairing, then try a bit more, and then decide. Find where pairing is useful and when it's not for you in your context, for your product, and with your team.

Pair programming has a lot to do with trust, as we consider the code we write a part of our intimate work. Letting someone in can feel intrusive, and that is why all the best practices we just discussed can make a huge difference to our success in pair programming. We deal with people, and social skills, interesting dialogues, and a positive state of mind are factors that always increase the trust in your pair. We'll next look at things you should not do when you are pair programming.

Pair programming anti-patterns

Particularly during your first interactions, pair programming can seem weird and potentially confrontational. I have seen so many people who have never paired before enter and argue, and their conversations turn impolite. You don't want that to happen when you are pairing. All your willingness to try something difficult vanishes and your energy gets funneled toward a sterile discussion.

In this section, we will discuss things that I wouldn't recommend doing when pair programming. This is because they are annoying, create frustration, and can even cause anger. Be careful when you are that person doing the things we are about to discuss, and try to correct yourself. Or, when you observe someone doing these things, give them some feedback on how to improve, but treat the matter with care and empathy.

Managing distractions

We can be faced with so many distractions when pairing: our phone, our tablet, a chat, an email, a colleague's joke, and more. When you are distracted, you are not pairing. Your partner will probably feel as though they are solo programming but with a person who gets involved from time to time and doesn't really help.

Try to remove all distractions for the duration of the pairing session. Of course, you can take an urgent phone call, as nobody should be bothered by that. However, anything more than that is a distraction, and it can hamper your understanding of what your partner is doing. Additionally, it makes your partner lack the natural support of pair programming.

Centering the monitor

Very often, I notice partners starting work on a laptop, and the owner of the laptop carefully sets the monitor in front of them, while the pair struggles to look at the screen with a twisted neck. For the navigator, it feels like they are less important than the driver. The navigator cannot have the full view of the monitor, and so, cannot fully help when needed.

Try to remember to center your monitor, even a small laptop, when starting to pair. Ask your navigator before starting, *"Is the monitor good for you, or do you want me to adjust it?"*, and then only if all is good, start pairing.

Dealing with the "I know it all" attitude

From a personal, untested statistic, 70% of people think they are better than the average. That idea boosts their ego. So, if you are one of those people, then you might think you know it all, and your partner cannot teach you anything. Usually, this attitude, which happens more often than you think with beginner pair programmers, is highly detrimental to the overall feeling of pair programming. It's not easy to start with an open heart, and then one of the pair starts dictating that this is exactly the solution, that is exactly what we need to do, without having any flexibility. The other person will either start getting annoyed and argue, or they might feel they are being bullied by their partner.

Try to ask for feedback at the end of each session. You might find that you were the person mentioned in the previous paragraph without even knowing it. Be open to suggestions, even if you know how hard it is to take feedback on how to improve, or even to take criticism. But remember that it's hard for all of us; we are all humans.

Addressing small pickings

You try thinking about the big picture, how to solve a particular problem, what the architecture is, what the design is, and suddenly your partner asks you if you should use tabs or spaces. Or why you use the mouse. Or that the color of the background is too yellowish. Essentially, they ask about anything that's marginal to the problem at hand. The details of working together are important. However, if we focus too much on small intricate details, we might not get anything done. And everyone has their own preferences.

Try to respect the other person's preferences when it comes to small details, and just focus on the important aspects of getting them done. Focus on the task at hand, and if you see something getting in the way, then address it. However, if that annoyance is not getting in the way of solving the current task, then please ignore it, even if it might be difficult for you as well.

These are a few of the typical pair programming anti-patterns that I have observed over the years. Try not to linger too much on any of these approaches. On the other hand, if you deal with people who do use these approaches, try to exercise patience since almost everything can be solved with some kind of feedback on how to improve.

Boosting productivity with remote pair programming

All of the techniques, styles, and practices that we have discussed in this chapter can also be used when working remotely. However, you do need some tools to enable remote pair programming, and we will focus on that during later chapters in the book.

Remote pair programming is wonderful because you can pair with people who are far away, in different countries, and on different continents. You can learn so much, and it is a lot easier than traveling to a conference or a workshop. You just have to open your computer, set up a few tools, and start pairing with someone who is sitting far away. You can also produce much better software if you pair for a shorter or longer period with someone who can help you in that particular situation.

The possibilities of remote pairing are endless. Your teammates can be everywhere. You can think about your usual team of 4 to 8 people, but you can also think about asking for punctual remote pairing sessions with people who aren't in your usual team. Maybe this could include people in your organization, but who are in separate city offices, and who could help you with that task. Alternatively, consider pairing with external consultants, technical coaches, or trainers to guide you when you feel you need a boost of energy, knowledge, or confidence.

Remote pairing is great, but it can somehow be more difficult than face-to-face pairing. Nevertheless, by following the preceding advice, with some practice and a commitment to openness, any challenge of remote pair programming can be overcome. You just need to try it, experience it, hang in there for a while, and it will be extremely rewarding for you and your team.

Summary

Pair programming is beautiful and pleasant, as long as it works well. In this chapter, we introduced pair programming techniques that are useful for different contexts. We need to adapt to the context in order to optimize the usage of pair programming. There is no one-size-fits-all approach because the situations where pair programming is used are so diverse.

Spicing the pair programming techniques with styles adds even more efficiency, but it also smoothens the rough edges of pair programming, making it even more agreeable. With pair programming styles, in the same way as pair programming techniques, there are variations and certain situations where each one should be used. The level of experience of the programmers involved in pairing is essential to pick the right flavor and the right spice of pair programming.

Additionally, to make things even better, we need to remember that we are dealing with people, and the way we communicate with each other is very important. Using an appropriate communication method for the context at hand massively improves the chances of a good pairing session, and it can lead to a boost in productivity. What is worse, you will want some more; it's addictive.

So, use pair programming techniques and styles, giving proper attention to details, communicate well, debrief often, and ask for feedback for constant improvement.

In the next chapter, we will get technical. We will explore which tools to use and how to use them in order to start building an efficient remote pair programming team.

Further reading

- The *Elastic Pair Programming* codecast from Adrian Bolboacă: `https://blog.adrianbolboaca.ro/2018/03/remotepairprogramming-ep-009-adi-ferdinando-elastic-pair-programming`

- *Overcoming Imposter Syndrome* by Gill Corkindale: `https://hbr.org/2008/05/overcoming-imposter-syndrome`

- *Empty Your Cup*: `http://wiki.c2.com/?EmptyYourCup`

- *Quiet: The Power of Introverts in a World That Can't Stop Talking* by Susan Cain: `https://www.goodreads.com/book/show/8520610-quiet`

Section 2: Remote Pair Programming

This section describes a hands-on, practical approach to starting to use pair programming in a remote way or in a distributed team.

This section has the following chapters:

- *Chapter 4, Using Pair Programming in a Distributed System*
- *Chapter 5, Remote Pair Programming Setup*
- *Chapter 6, Remote Pair Programming Specific Techniques and Styles*

4
Using Pair Programming in a Distributed System

Working in a distributed team can already be difficult. Pair programming in this context can also be a challenge.

Often, people consider that pair programming is not possible in a remote context. But not only it is possible, it is a good practice to have because the team will feel they are working together, as people working remotely often feel they work alone on individual tasks and stop thinking about the bigger picture. Or sometimes, they are just afraid it won't work when they're working in a distributed team. In this chapter, you will learn how to use pair programming when working from a distance, in a distributed team.

Furthermore, we will delve into the details of how to start organizing remote pairing, depending on the business requirements, level of expertise, knowledge sharing goals, and team member's personal preferences. Not all the pairing styles work in every context, even less so in a remote team, so you need to choose the right one for you and your context and learn how to choose the appropriate style.

You will not get a good organized remote pairing approach right from the beginning, which is why you need to reflect, change, and assess your current setup.

In this chapter, we're going to cover the following main topics:

- Organizing remote pair programming
- Performing regular retrospectives
- Improving the restrospectives continuously

Dealing with typical concerns about pair programming efficiency, we will learn about pair programming in a distributed system.

Technical requirements

I highly recommend that you have organized pair programming set up when you start using this tool for your team or for your organization. It will bring significantly better benefits than leaving everyone on their own and hoping they will start using pair programming.

Organizing remote pair programming

The steps mentioned in this section will help support your endeavor of starting remote pair programming. It's not a full, bulletproof plan, but we will take care of the main aspects, such as the reason for pair programming, operational details, social considerations, and how to apply all of these to a distributed team. Paying attention to the details will help you make a more effective transition to remote pair programming.

Let's begin with the first step.

The purpose of remote pairing

The first thing I ask my customers is: *why do you need X?*, and believe me, way too often I don't get a clear answer, or the answer is simply *I heard it's good, and we need it*. Unfortunately, it is most likely that they haven't heard, read, or understood enough about the technique, tool, or method they want to implement. Even worse, they believe the new thing can help in various areas, where, in fact, it can't help at all.

So, do yourself a favor and understand *why* you need remote pair programming, way before you start thinking about implementing it.

There are three batches of typical reasons – knowledge, operational, and social. These tell us why organizations want to start using remote pair programming. So, let's look at them one by one, and check which purpose fits you the best.

For **knowledge**, we have the following reasons:

- **Align knowledge**: We discussed this in *Chapter 1, Pair Programming and Its Necessity*, in the *Staff liquidity* section: we have some knowledge and we want the more experienced people to always work with someone else side by side in order to transfer knowledge and also add features.

- **Introduce new knowledge (new business domain, new tools, methods)**: In this situation, the team members would pair for a while with someone from outside their team who knows that business domain, tool, or method, which helps them gain new knowledge.

- **Add new people to an existing team**: This is a common situation when you want the newcomer to pair with all the existing team members and learn their tools, methods, and ways of developing software in that team.

- **Add existing team to an existing product or project**: This is similar to the previous example, but here, we affect the efficiency of another existing team, because they will pair with the new team in order to transfer knowledge, domain, tools, practices, and methods.

- **Start a new product or project**: In this situation, the reason to pair is to identify the best tools, methods, and practices that work for that new product or project. Pair programming is a good method for forming a team and making them perform well, quickly.

For **operational** reasons, we can make the following observations:

- **Minimize defects**: We have many defects, and most of them come from not paying attention to simple things. Solving a defect is expensive and takes a lot of time. So, it's better to start pairing and reduce the number of defects, thus increasing the productivity of the delivered features that passed the quality checks.

- **Minimize development and testing duration**: There are defects that are caught in the code review process, or by testers in the early stages. By pairing, we might minimize the number of defects that are created, and minimize the time that's spent back and forth between the code review and testing.

- **Minimize deployment duration**: When the deployment is done by (dev)ops outside the team, they keep struggling with the code that doesn't work. Then, we have team members pairing with the (dev)ops to understand how to write the code, package it, and make it work well for the deployment process.

- **Improve user experience**: In this situation, you'd like all the team members to pair with UX specialists, and also get to meet and pair more often with people from marketing, sales, or customer relations.

For **social**, we can make the following observations:

- **Increase team cohesion**: Especially when you form a new team, it's important for the team to start working as a whole as soon as possible. One important aspect of working effectively is that the teams establish their methods, tools, and ways of working together. There can also be a situation where teams have worked together for a longer period of time, without team cohesion. By starting to implement pairing on a regular basis, the team members can actively discuss, while working on concrete examples, which tools, methods, and practices to apply and when.

- **Eliminate silos between specializations**: A quite common situation that you see especially in big organizations in the testing department, the programming department, the ops department, and so on is people from these departments being able to work together, but their bosses need to harmonize their interactions. These interactions can be very different, depending on the product or project, and the people from different departments can collaborate on a regular basis.

This situation where people from different departments work together only after their bosses have agreed on, quite often, small details is a complete waste of time and effort when we're talking about knowledge work. This type of micromanagement is not only inefficient, but it also makes management so busy with the small things that they don't have the time and energy to work on strategy, development, and continuous improvement. That is the reason why we should start forming cross-functional teams that can make their own decisions, depending on their specific context. In this situation, pair programming is good because the different specialists can see how the other specialists like them, or teams with completely different focuses are working, and start understanding how to work together.

For example, a programmer might know what a tester is doing and what they need in order to start testing, and will adjust the needed information and build procedure to the tester's needs.

- **Transformation to self-managed team**: You have a team that works together, but they still have a team leader, a project manager, or a team manager of some sort telling them what to do. This type of micro-management is not at all effective in any type of knowledge work, software development included.

The context is somehow similar to the preceding example, but not that precise. You don't have silos anymore, but the team members are not independent yet. So, it's a good idea to start taking steps toward giving more and more responsibilities to the team. This means, first of all, by pairing, to understand what the usual activities are (analysis, programming, testing, deployment, and so on), and to start letting them make more and more decisions, together, as a team. Pairing can be used more widely in this situation, with Scrum Masters, Product Owners, Project Managers, and many other roles. We are not talking about pair programming but pairing to understand the management aspects of a software development team.

Depending on your purpose, with the most likely one of the previous list, you need to choose the appropriate remote pair programming techniques. But before that, please look back at the previous chapter, where we discussed pairing techniques and styles. Check out the following matrix to see which pair programming technique is appropriate in which situation:

Purpose/Technique	Driver - navigator	Pairing - trainee	Beginner - advanced	Beginner - beginner	Ping - pong
Align knowledge	✔	✔	✔	X	✔
Introduce new knowledge	✔	✔	✔	X	✔
Add new people to an existing team	✔	✔	✔	✔	✔
Add an existing team to an existing product	✔	✔	✔	✔	✔
Start a new product or project	✔	X	X	X	✔
Minimize defects	✔	X	✔	X	✔
Minimize development and testing duration	X	✔	✔	X	X
Minimize deployment duration	X	✔	X	X	X
Improve user experience	✔	✔	✔	X	X
Increase team cohesion	✔	X	✔	✔	✔
Eliminate silos between specializations	✔	X	X	X	X
Transform into a self-managed team	✔	✔	✔	✔	✔

Figure 4.1 – Choosing a pair programming technique, depending on the purpose

As you can see, you can decide which of the basic pair programming techniques to use, depending on your purpose. It's highly recommended that you start with just one purpose per team, and after a few weeks analyze your progress and choose the next step.

Now that we have a mechanism to decide which programming techniques to use for improvement purposes, we will add another variable to the equation: distributed teams. You will see that distributed teams can be varied, and that there is no one-size-fits-all solution.

Distributed team

When we say *distributed team*, it may mean different things. We are looking at how the team members can work together from the point of view of time and space. This means that do they share the same, or similar, time zones, and do they share an office or not? When you read about *similar time zones*, this means you can have 1, 2, or 3 hours difference, and you can have at least half of the day common working time. When you read about *different time zones*, this means you have a big time difference of about 5-10 hours, so you cannot digitally meet unless you change your working hours from day to night. Let's look at some scenarios:

- **Same time zone, common office**: The team members can choose if they work remotely or at the office. For example, you have everyone working in Paris, France; they have an office in Paris, and most of the time they work there, but they can choose to work from home, a coffee shop, or any other place.

- **Similar time zone, distributed offices**: The team members all work remotely, and they don't meet face to face. For example, you have a team that is distributed in Europe; you have a few people distributed in London, Winchester, Paris, Rome, Bucharest, and Sofia. They have a maximum of 2 hours difference between them. Everybody is working from home, a coffee shop, or any other place.

- **Different time zone, no offices**: The team members all work remotely. There is no office where they can meet. For example, you have people distributed around the globe; you have a team made of people in France, Germany, USA, India, South Korea, and Romania. They have many hours difference between them, so some of them might need to work nights and sleep during the days if they want to digitally meet.

- **Different time zones, distributed offices**: The team members work remotely, but in different time zones. You can have offices where the local team members can meet. For example, you have people in San Francisco, France, and Bulgaria who can go to their offices, in their corresponding cities, but they have many hours difference, so some of them need to shift their working hours toward the evening if they want to digitally meet. Please refer to the following matrix:

Distributed team type/action	Start remote pairing	Restructure the team
Same time zone, common office	✔	X
Similar time zone, distributed offices	✔	X
Different time zone, no offices	X	✔
Different time zone, distributed offices	X	✔

Figure 4.2 – Figuring out if your distributed team is ready for remote pairing

I don't know about you, but some years back, I never thought there could be so many types of distributed teams. And even more so, I never thought that the particularities about the types of distributed teams can be so important.

Why are these scenarios important?

How can you remote pair if you don't e-meet? That's the whole point of remote pairing. In scenarios where you have people who cannot meet, I would recommend restructuring the teams so that they can meet and have closer time zones, and only after that start remote pair programming.

It may happen that smaller groups in the same time zone will start forming their own set of practices and skills. This set of practices and skills might be very different in-between these groups that have formed. This is a big issue for a future moment when you would like to harmonize practices. I've seen this happen in many teams, and the efficiency was sinking very quickly, because the only thing the two fractured parts of the same team were doing was rewriting the code that had written by the others. This can happen, and it's not just an isolated case.

Deciding on the scope

Let's take two extremes: you only pair on selected tasks, or you pair on everything, always, no matter how useful pair programming is. I would say that neither of these situations is good.

A better approach is to pair on a scope, with clear guidelines. It's a lot better to have clear guidelines on how to choose a task where pair programming is useful than having someone micro-manage tasks and filter each smaller or bigger task for the team.

The following is an example of scope, depending on certain features and tasks:

Tasks/ features	All the tasks	Business tasks	Programming tasks	Testing tasks	Configuration tasks	Deployment tasks
Feature "X"	X	X	✔	✔	X	X
Features "X," "Y," and "Z"	X	X	✔	X	X	X
New features	X	✔	✔	✔	X	✔
Existing features (or code)	X	✔	✔	✔	X	X
Subsystem "T"	X	✔	✔	✔	X	X
All features	✔	✔	✔	✔	✔	✔

Figure 4.3 – Scope, depending on the features and tasks

By looking at the preceding matrix, we can see that pair programming isn't very effective for configuration tasks, and almost not at all for deployment tasks. On the other hand, for almost all the programming and testing tasks, pair programming is considered useful.

But this is just an example, of course. Analyze your context, build your matrix, ask for feedback from everyone involved, try it, get more feedback, improve it, get more feedback, and improve it again.

Duration

Pair programming can be exhausting. From my own experience, I can tell you that if you pair for a full day, without being used to all the intense thinking, talking, interactions, and explaining, it can get to you.

For many years, I have been and still am facilitating coderetreats, which are 1-day events where people can pair and learn from each other. They typically happen on Saturdays. One time, I got involved in organizing the **Global Day of Coderetreat**, where programmers from around the world would gather and share the same day to pair and learn from each other. *Jim Hurne*, my good partner in organizing this event always said, *Sunday is the post-coderetreat hangover*. So, after any full day of pair programming, no matter how experienced a pair programmer you are, you will still feel a hangover if you pair intensely for a whole day.

The following matrix is for programmers who aren't used to pairing. Take it with a grain of salt and treat it as a guideline rather than a rule. Discuss with people about their pairing duration and let them choose:

With Duration/ experience	Absolute beginner	Junior	Mid	Senior	Trainer/coach
30 minutes	✔	✔	✔	✔	✔
45 minutes	X	✔	✔	✔	✔
Pomodoro*	X	X	✔	✔	✔
Half day	X	X	✔	✔	✔
Full day	X	X	X	✔	✔
Consecutive full days	X	X	X	X	✔

Figure 4.4 – Recommended pairing duration, depending on programming experience

There can be situations when a junior programmer has paired before, maybe during college, university, or community event and user groups. In these situations, the preceding matrix changes.

Here, *Pomodoro = 3 sessions of 25 minutes*, with 5-minute breaks in between and 15 minutes of break at the end.

Pomodoro technique

In the 1980s, the Italian psychology student Francesco Cirilio found himself close to taking an exam without studying enough. Then, he thought he could at least learn for 10-minute intervals. He used a kitchen timer that was the shape of a tomato to signal when the 10 minutes had passed. In Italian, pomodoro means tomato. The technique worked for him, and after some refinement, he found that you need to have 30-minute intervals, where you work for 25 minutes and spend the remaining 5 minutes having a break. A break means getting up from your desk, moving around, and not opening your phone or other devices. After three or four intervals, it's time for a longer of at least 15 minutes.

Here are the core steps of the Pomodoro technique:

1. Create a list of tasks and choose the most important one to start with.
2. Set the pomodoro (timer) to 25 minutes.
3. Work on the task until the time is over.
4. Take a short 5-minute break.
5. After 3-4 pomodoros, take a longer break.
6. Start again from *step 1*.

The technique itself is very simple and efficient. Of course, you can tweak it; maybe you work better in 30-minute intervals, or maybe you need longer breaks. The preceding format is just something to start from, experiment with, and adapt to your personality.

Here is a set of guidelines that will make the pomodoro technique work for you:

- During a pomodoro, close all distracting tools (email, chat, and so on).
- Split your tasks into chunks that fit in a pomodoro, so that you see progress.

We cannot close the email and chat for the whole day, but we can have 1 or 2 hours per day to close any distractions and just focus on work. That means also having an agreement with your team on when you can have this distraction-free time, and how you signal them. For example, I would enter the team's chat and say: *for the next 2 hours, I will work on task X and will not be available, but for any emergencies, please send a text message to my phone.* So, you need to find the balance between working on your task, solo or in a pair, and being available to the team.

Over time, I have learned that there are many benefits to using the pomodoro technique. Here are some positive effects of the pomodoro technique:

- You feel a sense of continuous progress.
- Fewer distractions means getting more things done, as task switching doesn't work.
- Fewer estimation errors, as you can have a benchmark for how much time a task really takes, because the variation of interruptions is eliminated.
- Reduces the complexity of your work by slicing and dicing your tasks into smaller chunks.
- It's easier to continue work as you continue from a clear, partially finished state.

I always try to be a critic of all the tools and techniques I use and find their flaws, as nothing is perfect. Surprisingly for me, I didn't find any downsides to the pomodoro technique. Once I started using it, it was like a natural approach, and I cannot quit using it. Maybe you can find its flaws, as I am sure there are some, but I couldn't find any.

Schedule

When you start pair programming, it's typical to have a clear schedule, let's say micro-managed scheduling. But as time passes, you should leave this to the team more and more. There is no need for someone to create a schedule as the team gets used to the activity.

It may sound confusing, but there is also the opposite situation, although it's not that usual in my experience, but it happens when the teams can schedule their sessions from the beginning. Of course, this situation is far better than the first, but not that frequent.

In the following table, we can see the team maturity phases from the concepts presented by Bruce Tuckman for the stages of team formation. In short, he says a team has four stages that it passes through: forming, storming, norming, and performing.

Using your context, look at the following guidelines as to when it's appropriate to schedule pair programming sessions, depending on team maturity and how the work is managed by the team:

Team maturity/work management category	New team	Forming team	Norming team	Storming team	Performing team
Whoever is available now	X	X	X	✔	✔
Tasks assigned to team members	✔	✔	✔	✔	X
Tasks self-assigned by team members	X	X	✔	✔	✔
Featured assigned to team members	X	X	X	X	✔
Features self-assigned by team members	X	X	X	X	✔
Features pulled by the team when available	X	X	X	X	✔

Figure 4.5 –Team maturity and work management category

From the preceding table, we can observe the following:

- During forming everyone is polite and explores the new team, methods, tools, and so on.

- After a while, the team members usually start to argue about how to work together, hence the storming phase. It's essential that a team passes through this phase as fast as possible.

- After arguing about some rules, the team starts to understand how to work well together, hence the norming phase.

- After becoming proficient with their own ways, collaborating well, and improving their tools and methods, the team might start to perform.

On the vertical axis, we have methods of work management. Typically, with traditional project management, you have tasks for each person, and these tasks are assigned to them by some manager (team leader, project manager). When the team starts being more self-sufficient, the team members should be able to pick their own task, and negotiate about who should take which task. It's a process where the manager delegates the management of work items to the team. Of course, you need to do that when the team is ready; otherwise, you might get negative results. A more efficient way to do this is to have a person who is responsible for a feature, or user story, without looking at the small level of tasks. And going even further, instead of giving features to people, let them pull the features from a prioritized list when they are available.

Why is this important for pair programming? It sounds more like management than programming. Exactly: that's what it is. And organizing pair programming is a sort of management job.

Kickoff

A good practice is to start a remote pair programming initiative with a short meeting, where all the details are explained and discussed, and where any concerns are raised and answered. Someone needs to prepare this kickoff meeting, and the first thing to do is to look at all the preceding topics.

This meeting should not go on long. In fact, no meeting should go on for long. Try to limit the meeting to 45 minutes, though a 30-minute meeting sounds a lot better.

Let's pretend we are preparing this meeting together. We need to fill in the following sections so that we understand what we must do and how to start using pair programming. Please treat them as placeholders that you need to fill in.

Defining purpose

The following questions need to be answered to define the purpose:

- Why do we need to use (remote) pair programming?
- How will it help?
- What are the advantages of (remote) pair programming?

Defining a distributed team type

You need to provide an answer to the following:

- Are we fully distributed, or do we have an office?
- If we're distributed, what type of distributed team are we?

What is the business scope?

You need to answer the following questions:

- What do we need to develop by using remote pair programming?
- Are there things we want to develop only when we are pairing face to face?
- What are the guidelines?

What are the task types we should pair on? What is the duration?

You need to answer the following question:

- How long are the first few sessions?

What is the schedule?

You need to answer the following questions:

- Which the tasks/features/stories we will use to pair on?
- As a guideline, how much time of the day should we spend on pairing?
- Should we pair daily? Isn't that tiring?

Who are the trainers and/or coaches?

You need to answer the following questions:

- Do we need a trainer or a technical coach to get us through the first few phases?
- If we need a trainer or coach, do we have someone in the organization who can help?
- If we don't have someone in the organization, can we hire someone from outside the organization?

How do we start?

You need to answer the following questions:

- When do we start pairing?
- What are the tasks/features/stories we start with?
- Will all of us start at once, or just some of us?

Which tools do we use?

You need to answer the following questions:

- What are the tools we will use for pairing?
- What are the tools for remote pairing?
- Are there security recommendations on how to use the tools?

Improvement ideas

You need to take the following into account:

- Ask the team how to improve the presented plan.

Wrapping up

You need to do the following:

- Create a summary of the whole discussion.
- Close with the main improvement topics, if any.

You don't necessarily need to present this in bullet points, as I have done. The most important thing is that you answer the questions provided and consider all the aspects. Usually, I treat such meetings more like a very short summary, with a discussion with the team later. It's a lot more important to chat with the people there than to start giving commands on how things will be done from now on.

Concerns

With any new tool, technique, practice, and in fact with any change that comes, we start having concerns of all sorts. In the following sections, we'll cover the typical concerns of starting to use remote pair programming at scale in an organization.

Two people working on the same task is waste

This is the most common concern that I have ever heard of when pair programming was on the table. Usually, it comes from people that are used to looking at productivity as a function of time spent. In this mindset, if one person produces 100 screws per day, two people, working individually, produce 200 screws per day. With this view, it's impossible that two people who work together will produce more than 100 screws per day, so it's obviously waste. This mindset comes from the Industrial Age and refers to producing physical goods.

For knowledge work, we also need to shift our view to maintenance and changeability costs. It's not enough to measure just the immediate work results. It's not enough to measure just how many tasks a person finished per week. We also need to measure how many defects come from the quality assurance process, and how difficult it is to change the existing system. We also need to take into consideration how many defects the team produces while changing a system that was not thought about with changeability in mind.

The following is the simplistic view:

Business Analysis ->	Development ->	Testing ->	Deployment

Figure 4.6 – Simplistic development flow

The following is the correct view:

Business Analysis ->	Development ->	Testing ->	Bug fixing->	Deployment ->	Maintenance

Figure 4.7 – Realistic development flow

Looking at the two preceding images, bug fixing is extremely expensive, and maintenance is even more expensive. There is a study from IBM called *Relative Cost of Fixing Defects* that states a defect is six times more expensive to fix in the maintenance phase.

So, imagine you have a developer cranking out software, rushing to get it done, and is delivering it very fast. In this situation, you need up to six developers just to fix the defects of that one developer, in order to keep the system in a good, changeable state.

Now, imagine that you have two developers working in a pair the whole day. Their defects rate reduces to half, to be conservative. You only need three people for maintenance (that's still a bad ratio as *2 : 3 production : maintenance*). All in all, you have five people doing the work of six, and pairing. If the two developers would hone their pairing craft even more and end up having just 10% defects (that's closer to my experience for mature teams), then you would have two people in production and just one for maintenance. There you go: pairing doubled your productivity.

Pairing remote is not possible

I had this idea a long time ago. But we didn't have the tools and internet speed we have now. Remote pairing can still be a challenge if you don't set up your tools, and you don't shift your communication and pairing patterns a bit.

You are not in the same room, so you need to wait for the other person to finish what they have to say. You need to express this clearly, even with video enabled, because visual communication is a huge part of the communication bandwidth that we need in order to understand our interlocutor.

The good news is that everything else can be done and can work in a remote fashion. For some people, it is even nicer that they can stay in the comfort of their home environment, push a few buttons, and there you go – you can pair with anyone in the world. Think about how many options remote pairing can bring to you. There are so many brilliant developers in the world who, believe me, are willing to pair with you. So, remote pairing is a great opportunity for learning.

Maybe the more annoying part is starting to pair and getting used to the tools. After getting used to the tools (IDEs, add-ons, video, audio, and so on), you will see that things start to work well, with some tools quirks that you need to get used to. So, it's more about getting used to the tooling that exists. We will cover this in *Chapter 5, Remote Pair Programming Setup*.

Tester – How can I pair with a programmer?

You can put any other role, such as analyst, Ops, UX, and so on, instead of *tester* in the heading here. The issue is that people are not used to working with other specializations; everybody is so stuck in what they do, so they consider the others' activities are rocket science.

It's just a question of perspective, and nothing more. If you were told repeatedly that a tester should never work with a programmer because that's bad, you might start believing that.

I often heard the following story, especially coming from project managers: the programmer should never work with the tester, because the programmer will convince the tester to be more gentle with quality assurance and so more defects will pass through. It almost sounds like the testers are these gullible people who are constantly being tricked by programmers not to do their jobs. In my experience, I have never seen that in a cross-functional team where everyone pairs with everyone, never mind the specialization in the team. Even more, I learned that testers start understanding how every developer thinks and will look more thoroughly into the contexts that might generate defects. For example, I know I am terrible with conditionals, and I need automated tests for that. A tester might observe that and decide that all the conditional logic needs even more examination than usual. Well, that's how you increase productivity and reduce defects and waste: by pairing in-between specializations.

That little tale with programmers and testers is just an example. Anyone can learn from anyone. And we don't want to produce proverbial team members who can do everything necessary. We don't use pairing to produce a programmer who knows how to test, deploy, and write user stories. In fact, we need a wide range of pairing to have more empathy and increase the level of team understanding. In this way, after a period of time, we increase the overall efficiency of the team.

Good practices of pairing

Here is a list of good practices for pairing in a distributed team context. As usual, we will look at some frequent scenarios.

Choose a pairing style according to your context

You can choose a style for your team that suits your needs from the following:

- Mature team, working together for at least 1 year
- An experienced team, working together for a short time

- An experienced team consisting of a few juniors or more juniors, and a few experienced programmers
- Building a new team with only experienced programmers
- Building a new team consisting of a mix of seniors and juniors
- Building a new team consisting of more juniors and a few seniors

Next are the screens required.

Minimum of two monitors

You have two monitors: one for the code and one for your video conversation. In this way, you can have your partner *close* to you. It's easier to understand what your partner is saying when you see their face.

My ideal setup would be the following: one monitor for video, one for my code editor, and a third monitor to see my partner's remote desktop. You are not always doing work in the IDE. Sometimes, you need to work in a directory, change a configuration file in your settings, and more. It's very useful that both remote partners share their screen with each other, use a video camera, and also use an IDE that they can use together to edit and build the code.

Learn your tools

Whenever you start remote pairing, it's important to learn the tools before cranking the engine to start coding. Take a few days to understand the tool, how it works, and try it out.

Start a dummy project in your code editor, add it to your source control, and see what happens and how you can work well. Maybe ask a colleague to test this new remote system together, without the idea to get anything done, but rather with the tester's mentality to see how you can crash the tool. It's important to know beforehand how a new tool works, how reliable it is, and what the dos and don'ts are.

Commit messages

When you do (remote) pairing, only one of the partners will commit to the source control. And to be fair, it's important to acknowledge both partners involved.

The current source control systems only permit one committer per changeset. That is a drawback when we do pairing as two people have worked, and that information needs to be recorded in the changeset. The only solution for now is to use the commit message to say who the two partners who worked together are, what they have done, and all the usual commit message style that you use.

I would recommend that you have a standard commit message structure that everyone uses. In this way, all the commits are easy to follow and you can see in the commit message if it was the work of a person, a pair, or a group. If you don't understand what's going on in that code, you can ask not only the committer, but also the pair who was involved in creating that code.

Keep pairing session notes

During each remote pair programming session, I note things down in a notebook, or on a piece of paper. I like to take note of small tips and tricks that I learned from my partner, what I learned about tool usage, or how the session was overall.

Both partners keep notes from their point of view, and at the end of each session, they take 5 minutes to debrief. This debriefing is where you compare the notes the two partners kept. These notes are useful to keep for the regular retrospectives of remote pair programming; to remember what you learned, liked, didn't like, or felt during the remote pair programming sessions with your team.

Anti-patterns

After looking at good practices, we also need to look at anti-patterns; that is, the not-so-good practices when it comes to pairing in a distributed team.

Only senior programmers pair

In some organizations, I saw this behavior where the juniors were left with some boring, non-important tasks, while the seniors had fun with the new and shiny things. This is completely unfair, and to avoid such situations, it's a good idea to have an organized start to pair programming in a team. Everyone gets the same values of why we do this, how to pair, and all the information that we started this chapter with.

It's completely unfair and highly unproductive not just for that particular team, but for the rest of the organization. Senior programmers should also have a role of guidance and spend minimal time teaching juniors. They should give them a direction of what to do and what not to do.

No video connection

Video is important, as we humans communicate a lot non-verbally. It's not enough to hear what the other person is saying – it's also important to see how the other person is saying the words.

Use a good HD webcam. Make sure you have good light on your face (no strong light from behind you that will make your face all black), or the opposite, not having enough light in the room. Check your video and make adjustments to the position and light.

Bad sound

Sound is more important than video when you're remote pair programming. Your first focus is on the code and the code editor, the second focus is on what your partner is saying, and the third focus is their camera. It's not that the video part is not important, but that sound is a lot more important than video.

Make sure you have a high-quality microphone. A basic cheap headset is usually not enough. Aim to have a high-quality microphone in your headset as a mid-range solution. A top-notch solution is a podcasting microphone, or a shotgun microphone.

Never use your laptop's microphone; your remote pairing partner will hear your typing sound and it's annoying, tiring, and bad in all manners of speaking.

Don't use an omnidirectional microphone (it takes the sound equally from all sides), but rather a unidirectional microphone. Your laptop microphone is omnidirectional, so that's all the more reason not to use it.

After a few common anti-patterns, it's time to look at how to improve our pairing in the team. The anti-patterns we've covered so far are things to look for, especially in the first few retrospectives. So, let's learn how to organize and use the regular retrospectives to make pair programming an efficient and fun activity.

Performing regular retrospectives

One time, while teaching and coaching on Scrum implementation, a programmer asks me, *How often should we do the daily Scrum?* Well, the obvious answer is: daily. With retrospectives, the answer is not that obvious, so let's see how often, in which moment, using which methods to retrospect.

And don't forget the reason for retrospection: complaining and whining, without solving anything – no! The reason for spending time with retrospectives is continuously changing smaller or bigger aspects so that you can continuously improve.

How often we should retrospect

You need to retrospect more often when you start pair programming in the team. My typical recommendation for starters is to have a retrospective every week. After you stabilize your work, chat with the team and let them decide.

You can have planned retrospectives (for instance, every Tuesday at 14:00 or even every Tuesday at 12:00), but you can also have retrospectives when needed. I would recommend having a retrospective every 2 weeks in most cases. For the second version, when the retrospectives are only when needed, I would recommend using it only with experienced, mature teams. Use it with teams who are committed to their own continuous improvement process.

It's very important to have the retrospective marked in a team calendar where everyone is invited. Add reminders for 1 hour ahead of the meeting. Make sure that there is a retrospective facilitator who is not part of the team (Scrum Master, Team Leader, Project Manager, and so on).

Retrospective techniques

The simplest retrospective tool I use is colored sticky notes. But you are remote, so you need to use tools for remote retrospectives. Here are a few simple techniques for remote retrospectives.

Red – Green

Here is an example of how to go about this:

1. Open a shared document and write two headings: red (things that can be improved) and green (things that we like).

2. Ask everyone to start writing their ideas. Take 5 minutes, or until everyone is done. Typically, 5 minutes is enough.

3. Then, start grouping the inserted items. Some of them may be duplicated or have the same internal meaning. Some may be grouped because we talk about symptoms of the same problem, but they may be grouped because they are related (communication, tools, and so on).

4. After grouping them, you start voting in the group. Each team member has a few votes and can distribute the votes in any way among the groups. For a seven-person team, I would choose five votes per person.

5. Order the topics and start discussing the most voted one. While talking about that topic, distinguish two moments: clarifying the topic and finding solutions. It's not enough just to complain; you also need to find solutions.

6. Write the solutions down and find someone that's responsible for each solution. Only one, and no more or less than one.

And there you go – you can end the retrospective with a conclusion.

Starfish

You know the lovely, brightly colored starfish in the ocean? We use that shape, and we distinguish between the following areas: *more*, *keep*, *start*, *less*, and *stop*:

Figure 4.8 – Starfish
(https://en.wikipedia.org/wiki/Starfish)

Let's take a look at these terms in more detail:

- *More* means actions that we want more, but we are doing them.

- *Keep* means things that we are currently doing and should not change at all.

- *Start* expresses actions that we should do, and we aren't doing them at all.

- *Less* says that we are doing some activities, they are valuable, but we are doing too much, and they aren't bringing us too much value for the time we spend.

- *Stop* means stop doing some actions that we are doing because they don't bring us any value, and they might have a negative impact on our work.

Draw this starfish and ask the team to provide their opinion. Take 5-10 minutes to do this; usually, 10 minutes should be enough. Keep in mind the *keep* actions and discuss what needs to be improved for the other categories. You will group, vote, discuss, and come up with actions, as in the previous example.

Other techniques

I will not explain more retrospective techniques, as there are many more out there. You can read about them in more detail in the many books about agile retrospectives that have appeared on the market in the last decade.

There are remote tools such as Retrium for organizing remote retrospectives. But I am sure there are millions of online tools for retrospectives out there.

You can use tools such as Miro or Mural for digital whiteboards, and for remote visual collaboration. They are great tools that keep expanding, and they are very useful for retrospectives and more.

What happens after a retrospective?

This the most important question. You can have wonderful, open retrospectives, but if no changes occur after the retrospective, you can call it a waste of time and energy.

You have some actions that somebody must have sole responsibility for. This person needs to make sure the action will take place. It's like a manager with a very small and clear scope. It's not that the action needs to be performed by that person, but that the person is in charge.

So, change should happen after each retrospective; otherwise, it's just a sterile collective analysis meeting.

These were a few ideas about retrospectives. There are books that are only on this topic. I hope the information that's been provided so far will make you want to learn more. Now, let's look at some other complementary ways in which we can improve, after implementing retrospectives.

Improving the restrospectives continuously

Retrospectives are just a part of continuous improvement, as retrospectives are a snapshot of your perception of the team's practices at any given moment. We need to further analyze the results of the retrospective, take the improvement actions seriously, and start seeing how each of us needs to change personally to improve the whole ecosystem. We cannot change the system without changing our personal behavior little by little. That is why, more than retrospectives, we should also look into a few more topics, all of which we will cover in this section.

Analyzing the results

As you started with a clear purpose in mind, you can check, after a while, if you are on the good path or not. Let's say you started with the purpose of minimizing the number of defects, and you started pair programming with that in mind.

Make sure all the data is available to the whole team. A good idea is that the whole team analyzes the data and looks at how useful this new practice is, and then takes this as a scientific form of analysis, but don't forget about the personal, human type of analysis: personal introspection.

Personal introspection

It's important to get through data, time spent, time won, features delivered, defect rate, and so on. But it's also, or sometimes more important, to think about how we felt with remote pair programming.

An introspection about how everything happened, what we did, how we communicated; all in all, how well all the team members felt when working in a remote pair programming way.

Use the good practice, explained here, about keeping notes during each remote pair programming session. In this way, you can take some time and read over your notes, and then think better about remote pair programming as to how it helps you and how it could be improved.

Tools analysis

The same notes that were taken during the remote pair programming sessions can be very well used to make a tool analysis. We have many tools that we use for remote pair programming: video, audio, screen sharing, coding editor, coding environment sharing, and source control. All these tools have pluses and minuses, and we need to think about whether they are suitable for our needs and context.

These are just a few ideas about improving continuously. At moments when I discuss this topic with teams, there are usually a few people who believe that you can improve up to a point, and then you need to stop, because there is nothing more to improve. Unfortunately for some, and fortunately for others, the world is in constant change, and in a more rapid change than ever, so improvement never stops. Please look more into continuous improvement, as it is a topic that many management experts have written about in the past 70 years.

Summary

Maybe organizing remote pair programming was a bit more than you expected when you started reading this chapter. In this chapter, you learned how to use your current purpose of using it in distributed system and enhance it with pair programming, how to define your type of distributed team, which techniques and practices are useful for this type of distributed team, and how to constantly improve your setup. It's not an easy task, but it's also highly rewarding when you see people enjoying working together, wanting to work more in this way, and never wanting to go back to their old, solo programming ways.

Take all the information of this chapter and adapt it to your context. If you have a two-person team, you don't need a lot of organizing and structuring up-front. If you have five teams of nine people, and all of them were to start remote pair programming together, it's a totally different story. So, be flexible, adapt, and take the useful information for your context.

There are good practices and also things to avoid while remote pair programming. Try to keep those in mind, no matter how you start organizing how to remote pair program.

Working in a distributed team is challenging but rewarding. You can do so many interesting things with people who are close by, but are, in fact, far away. You can reach people who would have been impossible to reach without working in a distributed way. It's just about us to make the distributed team work well, and I am sure remote pair programming will make it easier, as it happened for me, and for many teams I have worked with.

In the next chapter, we will get more technical about non-programming aspects such as video, audio, screen sharing, IDEs, and so much more. You don't need to create your own video studio for remote pair programming, but it's useful to know about efficient remote video and audio.

Further reading

- *Coderetreat – Hosting and Facilitating*, by Adrian Bolboacă and Alexandru Bolboacă
- *Bruce Tuckman – Developmental sequence in small groups*: `https://psycnet.apa.org/record/1965-12187-001`
- *IBM research – Relative Cost of Fixing Defects*: `https://www.researchgate.net/figure/IBM-System-Science-Institute-Relative-Cost-of-Fixing-Defects_fig1_255965523`
- *Agile Retrospectives*, by Diana Larsen and Esther Derby
- **Retrium**, a tool for online retrospectives: `https://www.retrium.com`
- **Miro**, a digital remote whiteboard system: `https://miro.com`
- **Mural**, a digital workspace for visual collaboration: `https://www.mural.co`

5
Remote Pair Programming Setup

In the previous chapter, we learned how to use remote pair programming efficiently in a distributed team. Now, it's time to look at the technical aspects of remote pair programming. In this chapter, you will find many guidelines around which tools to use and how to use them.

We will go into detail about how to set up remote pair programming. We can have a basic setup just with the usual video conferencing tools. However, we can spice things up and make pair programming even better by using specialized tools that attach to the IDE and enhance the overall experience.

By the end of this chapter, you will be able to start remote pair programming. After completing all the sections, one by one, you will be able to add to your lists of tools and practices so that you are good to go. Also, you will learn how to effectively use the tools for great remote pair programming sessions.

In this chapter, we're going to cover the following main topics:

- Setting up video and audio
- Setting up screen sharing
- Setting up the **Integrated Development Environment (IDE)**
- Organizing source control rules
- Using two computers for coding and remote screening

Technical requirements

Before you start this chapter, you need to make sure you have set up your environment with the following:

- A good internet connection
- A fast computer: 8 GB RAM, a 2.7 Ghz processor with 4 cores, HD screen resolution, and a dedicated graphical card or an integrated graphical card to handle HD video
- Administrator rights or the ability to install software on the machine

Once you have everything in place, you can start learning how to set up remote pair programming.

Checking the internet connection

First, we need to make sure our internet connection is good enough. Depending on the tools we use, we might need more or less bandwidth, but we will surely need a stable connection.

Let's get technical. You need a connection that is stable at around 10 Mbit/s download and 5 Mbit/s upload. That is on average. It depends a lot on the tools you use, as some video conferencing or screen sharing tools will have better compression rates than others. If you want a mobile reference, a 4G mobile connection speed is what you need for a good remote pair programming experience.

Preferably, you should have a fiber optic connection. That will make your remote pair programming session seamless from a connectivity point of view. Still, even in this case, your Wi-Fi router can cause problems. Once, I was pairing with my laptop really close to the Wi-Fi router that the laptop could even touch it, and even then the connection was unstable at times. Only after I found a wire and plugged my laptop in did I start having a nice, stable, speedy connection.

In the following sections, you will find a few ways to get a good internet connection that is sustainable for remote pair programming. The first option is the best; the rest of the options tend to have more and more inconveniences.

Using a cable connection

My first choice is always to use a **cable connection**. It's a lot more stable, brings better speeds, and fewer packages are dropped. I know we live in a wireless world, but the truth is that you need many wires to have a good wireless system.

My preferred approach is to plug the computer(s) I use for remote pairing into a router or an Ethernet switch. You don't need a fancy equipment; typically, anything on wire is more reliable than wireless.

Using a Wi-Fi connection

Wi-Fi comes as the second-best option for remote pair programming. It's important to have at least 60% signal strength if you want to have video, audio, screen sharing, and a shared IDE.

Use an internet speed checker to see your Wi-Fi speed. If you don't have a good enough speed, then try to move closer to the router. The Wi-Fi connection is very sensitive to concrete and iron walls, and sometimes even a minor change in position might increase the signal strength from not good to good enough.

Using a portable router

When I am away from my environment, whether traveling or in another office, I have a **portable router** with me. Many times, I have used the internet plug in my hotel room to get significantly better internet than what's provided by the hotel Wi-Fi. Sometimes, when I'm allowed, I use the same portable router in a client's office. It's always better to be close to your own Wi-Fi.

It's not at all ideal, but quite often, it's a better solution than an unreliable Wi-Fi connection. If you have good Wi-Fi, don't consider this option, as it's more like a hack to keep you going.

Having a bad connection is a nuisance. It defocuses you from the main task, while trying to see if the other person can hear you, see you, and work with you. That is why having a good internet connection is an essential aspect of the whole remote pairing experience. My conclusion is: wire is the best.

We've covered the basic internet needs to enable remote pair programming, so now, it's time to look at how to use this internet connection for video and audio remote conferencing.

Setting up video and audio

Before we start coding, we need to hear and see each other. Working remotely implies more setup than working face to face. So, let's see what we need to do in order to create a good virtual experience for pair programming. First we set up the video.

Setting up video

A good video connection will increase the feeling of closeness to your remote pair partner. That's why it's important to have high-quality video. Of course, the quality of the video connection is highly dependent on the internet connection. Quite often, when I'm pairing across the seas, at high distances, the video connection isn't great, even though we both have high-speed fiber optics at home. That is why the tool we use for video connection is also important. Some are better than others, and you can see the difference between how well you see your pair partner on a high-distance video connection.

There are so many video conferencing tools out there, but there are some that are more popular. It's important, especially if you're working with many people from different organizations like me, to be flexible. If you work with your colleagues from the same organization, you most probably have your go-to system already set up. Nevertheless, it's important to see how ideal video conferencing tools would behave. Also, we will look at the pros and cons of some existing video conferencing tools currently on the market.

The ideal video conferencing tool should have the following:

- A stable video connection
- HD video by default
- A **frames per second** (**FPS**) rate of at least 24
- Good compatibility with any operating system, both on desktop and on mobile

Let's see which are the most used video conferencing tools, and some pros and cons for each of them, from my personal experience:

- **Zoom**:

  a. Pros: Really good HD connection, easy to set up and start, very stable, and a good FPS.

  b. Cons: Privacy is not ideal. At the time of writing, Zoom has a number of well-documented security issues.

- **Skype**:

  a. Pros: People are used to it and it's easy to start.

  b. Cons: Not very stable quality, often pixelated image, and HD is not stable, as it often downgrades SD quality.

- **Google Hangout/Google Meet**:

  a. Pros: Many people are used to it, easy to start.

  b. Cons: Stable quality only on shorter distances, often pixelated image, it supports only HD (720p), and not full HD (1080p), it often downgrades the HD quality to SD quality.

- **Jitsi**:

  a. Pros: Good quality, stable, and good privacy as you can host it on your server.

  b. Cons: Not many people know about it; you need to set your own server, which is a lot more complicated than installing a tool or an app.

- **BlueJeans**:

  a. Pros: Good quality, stable, good HD quality, and good FPS.

  b. Cons: Not well known and you need a subscription to use it.

After setting the video, we need to check the lights.

Checking the lighting

It's nice to see the other person's face as clearly as possible. For that, we need to get technical about light positioning. The instinctive approach is to open the camera and start the video call. But there is more to it than that. It's a good idea to look at your image in your video conferencing tool and see if you have good, balanced colors on your screen.

What I will tell you is that the following are the basics of lighting setup, so if you want to learn more, you have a whole new world opening up for you.

Here is the ideal setup for your lighting, considering you work at a desk. You need to have the following:

- **Front-left diffused light and front-right diffused light**: Both these lights need to have the same intensity; that intensity depends on the distance from the light source to you. For a small office I use one light bulb, but for each of the sources, a 1000 lm bulb, and a neutral light color of 4000K.

- **Backlight**: This light creates depth in your image. Typically, a yellow, warm light is the best solution. For a small office, I use a light bulb of 800 lm and 2,700K light color.

There are some situations when your pair partner won't see you at all, because of bad lighting. Here are those situations:

- **Strong backlight**: This will make your face look dark. In photography, it's called *contre jour* (from French), meaning against light. In this situation, your image would look like a silhouette in the video.

  You need to dim the backlight, and make sure you have a front light as well to counter the backlight.

- **Strong front light**: This will make your face look very bright. In photography, it's called burnout, meaning that the image looks like it's burning. In this situation, your face may look washed out because of the excess light and your expressions can't be observed.

  The opposite of the previous situation, you need to dim the front light and set a backlight to counter the front one.

- **Strong lateral light**: This is typical when you are in a sunny room with many windows and the sun shines on your face from a lateral window. Usually, you just need to use some curtains to diminish the strong lateral light.

This may sound like a lot of work, but it's not that complicated. I bought three cheap lamps, some bulbs, and everything was done with an expense of a few euros. Please have a look at these lighting details and see how much of a difference good light makes when you pair with someone. If you can see their facial expressions, with HD image quality, you can almost feel that you are in the same space. Our brain appreciates this apparent closeness, and we can work with a lot more productivity. Good lighting is an aspect worth taking into account.

With that, you have learned about how to use light in the context of remote pair programming, or a remote video conference. Now, it's time to choose your video camera and put it to use.

Choosing the camera

Today, almost everyone has a webcam in their office or at their home. They are a simple, easy solution to get started with a remote meeting, or with a remote pair programming session. But this versatility is paid off by their lack of quality.

When I first started recording videos and pairing extensively, I thought any webcam would be good enough. But with time, I learned that you need more than a basic webcam from a basic laptop, if you want to have a good experience. Here are the basic characteristics for a camera that is appropriate for remote pair programming, or for any remote video meeting:

- Full HD (1080p or 1080i)
- 30 FPS
- USB/HDMI output

Depending on how much you want to invest, there are two basic choices, with the first we'll cover being better and a lot more expensive. So, let's look at each.

DSLR/mirrorless camera

You cannot get great quality with any webcam for the simple reason that a semi-professional or professional camera would have a bigger sensor that can get more detail through its lens. This option is a lot more expensive than the second one, probably around 10 times more expensive.

Here are my top choices for this category, with the best mentioned first:

- Panasonic Lumix DMC-GH5 with Lumix 12-60mm f/3.5-5.6 G Vario Power OIS
- Fujifilm XT-3 with XF16-80
- Canon PowerShot G7 X Mark II

What's more, you cannot just connect your semi-professional or professional camera directly to your computer. You need a video capture card that can transform the HDMI signal into a USB signal so that your computer will think it's dealing with a webcam. Not all capture cards are compatible with all cameras, and not all capture cards are compatible with all operating systems. The joy of *plug-and-play*!

Here is a list of my favorite video capture cards. The one at the top is the most reliable, but that also depends a lot on your camera. The others can be just as good if you have a good match between the camera and the capture card:

- **Epiphan AV.io HD or 4K**: Extremely versatile capture card. It works on almost everything. Its only disadvantage is its price, which can be too much for any programmer who wants to pair a couple of times.

- **Elgato Cam Link**: This is a small capture card that looks more like a USB stick. It works well with some cameras, but not at all with many cameras. You need to check for compatibility with your camera before buying it.

- **Magewell USB Capture HDMI Plus**: A lot more expensive than the previous option, but much more stable. It is compatible with many cameras, but still, the price is quite high.

And after all the aforementioned gear, you need a tripod for your camera. Your camera cannot sit on its own.

Webcam

If you don't have the money to invest in a professional solution, or you just don't want to, there is always the webcam option. You can get a good enough image with a webcam; you just need to take more care about the lighting in your room. A good camera will compensate for some slip-ups with lighting, while a webcam will be very sensitive to bad lighting.

Here are my favorite webcams:

- **Logitech C920e Pro**: Really good image, even in bad light conditions. It's a bit pricey, but it will do the job for a long time after you have bought it. Very stable, with no issues.

- **Microsoft LifeCam HD-3000**: Really good camera, with color correction and a good price for the image quality it has.

- **Logitech C922 Pro**: Probably the best camera on this list, but a lot more expensive than the others.

What is very convenient about a DSLR/mirrorless camera is that you can zoom in/out on yourself and on your face. Some webcams have this functionality to zoom in, but it's often a software zoom that makes the image quality not that great, and a lot more sensitive to bad lighting. Because you want your face to be seen clearly by your remote pairing partner, it's important to zoom in on your face. That is one more reason why I would go to the DSLR/mirrorless camera option, if I were to pair for a considerable amount of time.

> **Note**
>
> I am not at all an expert in videography, but I can tell you what I have tried, and what has worked for me in my experience as a remote pair programmer and video podcaster.

Understanding the camera's position

We have touched a bit on this topic, but now, it's time to get into the details. How often have you met virtually with someone and their camera was on their chin and neck, or you could see them from the side, without understanding much about what you were seeing? I have had these experiences, and many others like it.

You want your camera to stay in front of you. Often, with a laptop, that's not very obvious, because you want to have a good view angle on your monitor, and that often means that your camera will not be on your face.

It's important that you position your camera so that it's on your face, because that is the image you want your remote pair partner to see. You can set it so that a bit of your upper body is seen, but it would be a mistake to position it so that you are very zoomed out, a long distance from the camera.

Here are some unwanted settings for the camera:

- Far away
- Very close to your face, so that your face is only partially seen
- Frontal, but at an angle

So, take the time to set your camera to a good position, as it will make a big difference for your remote pair partner. Ask your pair partner to do the same; that is, to position their camera so that you can see them. Like anything new, it will take a while to get used to checking the correct camera position, but after a while, it becomes second nature.

Good camera position is one of those simple things that makes a huge difference in the overall remote pairing experience.

Checking the audio

When we talk about virtual remote communication, we often believe video is the most important. But, in fact, audio is more important than video. For a good remote pair programming experience, it's essential to have good audio quality, as there's a big difference between a nice, crystal-clear sound and a tiring, straining sound.

You know the experience is bad when you take your headphones off and you feel dizzy and tired after an hour of remote pair programming. If you get up and you feel like your normal self, then it means the audio was good, so keep it up.

Introducing audio

Let's get technical about audio. This is a very short introduction to microphones and how they work. I have tried to explain only the bare essentials. For more information, please study more, as there are plenty of good resources out there.

They are split into the following two categories:

- **Omnidirectional**: Your embedded laptop microphone is omnidirectional. It is a microphone that can hear from all directions, 360 degrees. It's a good microphone for catching sounds in a meeting room, where you have more people present, or in a stadium to hear the background noise. It is highly impractical for remote pair programming, as your pair partner gets to hear your keystrokes, sounds from outside if you have your window open, or sounds from your house/office if other people are around working.

  This type of microphone is exactly what you need to avoid, in order to have mercy on your pair partner and spare them a headache.

- **Directional**: This is a microphone that can detect sound only from one direction. Depending on its characteristics, it can have a wider or narrower spectrum, between 180 degrees to just 40 degrees. The former is called a **cardioid pattern** because the spectrum graph looks like a heart. The latter is called a **supercardioid** or **hypercardioid** pattern because it will only get sound in front of it.

  You need at least a cardioid microphone for remote pair programming. You will have less background noise, a clear sound, and with a good-quality microphone, your partner will feel like you are very close.

Next, we choose the mic.

Choosing a microphone

The embedded laptop microphone is the worst option for remote pairing or virtual conferencing. They are omnidirectional and extremely small, so they don't capture your voice very well. It will get the mid-range of the audio spectrum, which also means a lot of noise if you are in a bigger room, in a room with an echo, or in an office with other people. These microphones are typically placed near your keyboard, or near your embedded webcam. When you type on your laptop, the other person hears a strong typing sound, as if you were using an old typewriter directly on their head.

After the very condensed description provided here, you now know why you need a good microphone. The best option was mentioned first. But also, it's the most expensive option. Choose wisely, depending on how much time you spend remote pair programming, as well as your budget. We'll look at the best options in the following sections.

Podcast/broadcast microphone

For these microphones, you need an external sound card that can connect a professional XLR audio plug. Also, you need an XLR audio cable to connect the microphone to the external sound card, and a microphone stand. These microphones are bigger, so they can filter the sound a lot better, to give crystal-clear sound even in big rooms with an echo.

On the other hand, these are expensive microphones that cannot sit somewhere on a desk. You can pay from 50€ to 300€ for such a microphone. Furthermore, the external sound card costs from 50€ to 200€ as well, while a good short XLR cable is around 10€ to 30€.

You can find my favorite gear for each entity in the following sections. At the top is the best professional gear, which is the most expensive, while toward the bottom, you can find very good semi-professional gear. Of course, my options might be controversial, because we all like our own tools. But this is a great place to start, without spending hundreds of hours researching, like I did.

For *microphones*, we have the following options:

- **Electro-Voice RE20**: An old-timer professional microphone that's been used for more than 40 years in radio stations around the world. It filters the hum created by electrical equipment and has an internal pop filter and shock mount.

- **Shure SM7B**: It is called Michael Jackson's microphone, as he popularized it because he used it for recording his Thriller album. It's a professional microphone used extensively by podcasters; a microphone created for voice.

- **Rode Broadcaster or Rode Procaster**: As the name suggests, the latter is a microphone created for podcasting. There are technical differences between them, but for our purposes, they are the same. Both catch a nice, crisp voice, and you will sound like you are broadcasting from a professional radio station.

- **Behringer C-1**: A budget option for a voice microphone. It's a lot cheaper than the others, but it can give you all the sound clarity you need for remote pair programming. There is also a USB version called Behringer C-1U, which has an integrated USB sound card.

For *external USB sound cards*, we have the following options:

- **Yamaha AG03**: The almost-professional solution to sound broadcasting, or sound recording. You can adjust the highs and lows, and you also have a voice compressor. The compressor makes your voice sound much more like you're on the radio, moving the very high and the very low sounds toward the middle audio spectrum. Because of this, loud noises are diminished, and low whispers are amplified.

- **Focusrite Scarlett Solo MKII**: It's the semi-professional option for single microphone broadcasting, typically used by podcasters in a small studio. It has a crisp sound, without background noise. It's easy to set up, and no drivers need to be installed.

- **Behringer Xenyx 302USB**: The budget option for a mini-mixer that also allows you to set the high and low sounds, making your voice sound great and taking advantage of the qualities of your microphone.

- **Behringer U-Phoria UMC22**: This is the budget option for a sound card. It doesn't have a crisp, studio sound, but it's good enough for any remote pair programming session. It's easy to set up, without the need for drivers, on any operating system. You can use the gain (sound output) from this to amplify the microphone, and the headset plug to get decent audio from your pairing partner.

- **USB external microphone**: These microphones are the compromise between a decent quality, having a piece of gear with wires, and price. They are very good for remote pair programming, recording podcasts, and attending remote meetings. You only need the microphone and a stand for it.

Here is the list of *USB external microphones* that I like, with the best one at the top:

- **Blue Yeti Studio Blackout**: A good option for beginner podcasters, and for long-time remote pair programmers. You need to set it up in front of your keyboard, close to your mouth so that it will mainly pick up your voice. It has a gain and a speaker knob. It's easy to set up, and you're ready to pair program quickly and easily.

- **Rode NT-USB**: A simple microphone, with good audio quality. No gain or volume controls, so you need to know how to place it to remove any unwanted sound, while still keeping your voice clear for the other end of the line.

- **Behringer C-1U**: The budget option for USB microphones; it's easy to set up and, most importantly, a lot better than your embedded laptop microphone.

For a *headset with a microphone*, for me, there isn't a lot of difference between the different types of headsets with microphones. In my experience, the ones that are more expensive have better sound quality for both the speakers and the microphone. There is a wide range of headphones with microphones from 20€ to 300€. But if you want to spend 300€, why not choose a good microphone, and a good headset with obviously better quality overall?

While the professional and semi-professional options for microphones with external sound cards are the best, it's not that easy to move them around, and you don't want to keep them in an open-space office. A microphone like that can break easily if it falls on the floor, so you need to be extra careful. The USB microphone is a good compromise: good sound quality, easier to carry around, and not that expensive. The headset with a microphone is, for me, just a last-resort situation. It's not that great; those microphones don't deliver very good quality, and I would avoid them for any remote pair programming session that lasts for more than 30 minutes.

Now, you have an idea of how to choose your microphone and can order one. Maybe you already have a microphone and you can start using it. However, before you start your remote pair programming session, it's time to learn how to position it so that your remote pairing partner will hear you as if you are in the same room.

Positioning your microphone

When we're talking about sound, we say that the source needs to be close to the microphone. In this case, because we aren't playing an instrument, the source is our mouth. So, it's important to place your microphone as close to your mouth as possible, while also taking care not to tilt it toward the keyboard, because the clacking of the keys will get through much more than it should. Some microphones are louder, while some are quieter. Depending on the microphone you buy, you might need to speak really close to it, like radio people do.

For a headset microphone, take care not to position the microphone in front of your mouth, because your pairing partner might think they're pairing with Darth Vader, with a heavy breathing sound. Always position your microphone lateral to your mouth, but close enough that it catches your words.

Use headphones, not loudspeakers

In order to avoid audio feedback, it's essential to use headphones. When you use a laptop's loudspeakers, or any external loudspeakers, it often happens that your pairing partner will hear themselves in an echo. It depends on what virtual conferencing tool you use, as some are better and some are worse at removing sound feedback. But still, it's good practice to always use headphones.

While we're talking about headphones, let's see what headphones are the best to use for a long remote pair programming day. There are three main types of headphones, and the most appropriate for remote pair programming is mentioned first:

- **Over ear**: These cover the whole ear and often have noise reduction functionalities. They need to be comfortable, as some of them don't fit very well on the head or create tension on the ear lobe for a person with big ears like myself. The best ones aren't necessarily too expensive; it's mainly the ones with noise-canceling functions that are.

- **On ear**: These stay on top of the ear, but you can still hear sounds near you. They don't offer any noise reduction. Also, because they stay on the ear, they can create some pressure on it and they will feel uncomfortable after a few hours.

- **In ear**: These headphones are the most inappropriate for long-time pair programming because they heat inside your ear and start being highly uncomfortable after a few minutes or so. Also, studies have been conducted showing that bacteria levels increase dramatically after using in ear headphones for tens of minutes. So, for your health, I recommend that you do not use these if you have a long pair programming session.

Mute pairing

During code retreats, I sometimes ask the partners to pair without speaking for a while. It's a fun exercise that shows how important oral communication is between programming partners. The rules are simple: you need to communicate through code, and you aren't allowed to talk or make gestures. You aren't allowed to use your text editor as a chat. All communication should be done by writing code.

After 45 minutes of mute pairing, the partners debrief. Here are the most common things to hear after this kind of exercise:

- We wrote more code because we talked less; we didn't argue before starting.

- The code we wrote was easier to understand because we focused more on communicating through code.

- It was difficult to make strategic decisions because we couldn't talk.

I do recommend that you try mute pairing as a fun exercise for a short while and see how that works out with your pairing partner. After that, you will give a lot more importance to what you say, and maybe to what you shouldn't say.

When we are remote, verbal communication is a bit more difficult than when we are face to face. You sometimes need to wait in line to say something, the connection interrupts itself, you cannot hear your pair partner very well, and so on. So, because of these conditions, it's even more important to be extra careful with what and how you communicate verbally to your pairing partner.

To conclude, please make sure you use the remote voice channel to keep communication short and effective, and always with a focus on advancing the work at hand.

You might have found a new world in this audio and video section. After many details that I struggled to keep as short as possible, you have all you need to get started. And now, it's time to look at another important aspect: how to choose your IDE, and how to set it up for remote pair programming.

Setting up the IDE

After much non-coding and technical information, it's time to get closer to what we are really doing: programming. Most programmers I know use an IDE to edit code, but I will also offer simpler editor options for remote pair programming. Of course, some IDEs are tightly coupled to a technology stack, though there are more and more IDEs that can support more technologies. I will go through the main IDEs for the main technologies. You can use at least one of the following for almost any technology stack out there.

Using an IDE with a remote pair programming add-on gives you the best experience, as you feel like you are coding together. There is another option, and that is to pair on a remote shared desktop, as you will see in the next section. I would recommend the second option only if you have a very short task, such as showing something for 10-15 minutes. Otherwise, remote pairing on a remote shared desktop is cumbersome, annoying, can lag, and has many more nuisances. So, that's why the normal solution is to use a text editor or an IDE to work on the code together with your pair partner, like you would do if you were next to each other.

For smooth remote pair programming, a code editor needs a few key functionalities. Before choosing the editor and its extensions that enable it to work well for remote pair programming, please look at the following checklist.

Key editor functionalities

Let's take a look at key editor functionalities:

- **Live editing**: Both partners need to be able to edit the code at the same time, either in the same file or in different ones. Sometimes, you will want to parallelize work and edit different files at once.

- **Follow pair**: Wherever the driver is putting their cursor, the navigator will automatically see their cursor in the same spot. This is a very nice feature that makes you focus on what is going on, and not on *where are you working now?* When the driver moves from one file to the other, you should see the other file, or be notified visually that the driver is working in a different file.

- **Unfollow pair**: This is quite obvious – it's the opposite of the previous option. Sometimes, you don't want to follow the driver, because you will be working on different things for a while. Often, this is very useful for basic, trivial tasks that can be parallelized by the pair partner and performed twice as fast. After a split in activities, I always recommend a short debrief so that you both know what you have done.

- **Sync new files**: Any new file that's added to the project should be visible to the other pair partner. As you often add new files when refactoring, either to add a new feature or improve legacy code, you would like that file to be visible to both partners.

Now, let's look at the best IDEs for remote pair programming.

Best IDEs for remote pair programming

The tool we use the most when programming is our code editor, or our IDE. Our preferred editor is not always a good choice for remote pair programming. Some code editors have made enhancements to support remote pair programming natively, though there are some add-ons that help some code editors work in a remote pair programming context. In the subsection, you will learn what you need from a good code editor to work well in a remote pair programming context, and what tools are now on the market that will make your life easier with remote pair programming.

Intellij IDEA

This is probably one of the best editors, with high capabilities for code editing, refactoring, integration, and so many other things. It works with multiple technologies, as follows:

- Clojure
- CloudSlang
- Dart
- Elm
- Erlang
- Gosu
- Groovy
- Haskell
- Haxe
- Java
- Julia
- Kotlin
- Lua
- Perl
- Python
- Rust
- Scala
- XML
- R
- ActionScript
- CoffeeScript
- Go
- HTML
- JavaScript
- PHP
- Ruby/JRuby

- SQL
- TypeScript

To make it work for remote pair programming, you need to add the plugin called **CodeTogether**, native from JetBrains. The plugin enables end-to-end encryption and on-premises hosting.

Visual Studio Code

Despite Microsoft's reputation for building tools only for their programming languages and technologies, Visual Studio Code is a great exception to that rule. And the tool is quite good, stable, and nice to use. It works with almost every major technology, including the following:

- .NET Core
- C#
- Node.js
- JavaScript
- JSON
- HTML
- CSS
- TypeScript
- Markdown
- Powershell
- C++
- Java
- PHP
- Python
- Go
- T-SQL

For me, Visual Studio Code was a pleasant surprise from Microsoft. I consider it the most versatile code editor built for remote pair programming at the moment. The reason I consider it to be so good is that it supports almost all the major programming languages. Also, the editor can be enabled for remote pair programming with a coding extension called **Live Share**.

Furthermore, you can use the additional functionalities of **Live Share Audio** to remove the need for another audio-conferencing tool, and **Team Chat**, to be able to chat while coding. The chat is very useful for sending various code snippets, configuration details, implementation details, and so on.

The only thing that Visual Studio with Live Share is lacking is the video conferencing option. If it had that, you wouldn't need a second tool for it anymore, and you could have an integrated coding and audio-video conferencing environment.

The issue with screen sharing remains, as I would also like to be able to see what the other person is doing outside the editor. So, an extra screen sharing tool is needed anyway, but the setup becomes simpler with Visual Studio Code.

CLion

We covered most of the programming languages with the editors in the previous sections, but C++ is always special. From my experience, CLion is the best IDE for C++ that I know. They are working to extend its refactoring capabilities, which are needed for C++ and not at all present in the other C++ editors. You can use Visual Studio Code for C++, but if you are a professional full-time C++ developer, you know why you need a dedicated editor for C++, C, and Objective-C.

Code with me is the best plugin to use with CLion to enable remote pair programming for C++. Actually, it's the only option, besides Floobits. C++ has always been misrepresented in the world of IDEs, code editors, refactoring, and other helpful tools. Now, I'm glad that C++ programmers can also join the remote pair programming world, with tools that are appropriate and easy to use.

Vim, Tmux, and SSH

Strangely enough, Vim is the first tool I used for remote pair programming. For any Vim lovers, it's the go-to approach for remote pair programming. Vim is difficult to learn, but once you get the bug, you cannot stop learning more and more about it. Extensions, custom extensions, scripts, shortcuts – you name it.

The versatility of this system is huge. I would need to provide a very long list of the programming languages out there that you can use with Vim. With this versatility comes the price of learning Vim, setting it up, making it work, understanding what doesn't work, and why.

Tmux is an open source terminal multiplexer for Unix. Of course, you can use it on Windows as well, and you can use Vim on Windows as well. Basically, Tmux enables remote control over a terminal. It's the simplest and fastest no-lag remote pair programming option out there. There are no big images to send over the wire; there are just very small commands that are sent over an SSH tunnel. So, security and privacy are embedded into this simple but efficient system.

Best editor plugins for remote pair programming

Besides the code editors that have their native plugins to enable remote pair programming, there are also independent plugins that enable remote pair programming on a few editors that are compatible with the plugins.

Code Together

It works with the following editors:

- IntelliJ IDEA
- Eclipse
- Visual Studio Code

What is amazing about this tool is that you can work across IDEs. You can have Eclipse, while your remote pairing partner can have IntelliJ. You will be able to remote pair without any issues. It's a really nice tool, but I hope that it will integrate with more and more IDEs in the near future.

The following are the pros:

- Easy to start with and set up
- Live editing
- Follow pair
- Unfollow pair
- End-to-end encryption
- Works across IDEs, and across IDE versions

The following are the cons:

- Subscription-based
- Doesn't support many IDEs

Floobits

This works with the following editors:

- Emacs
- Sublime Text
- Neovim
- IntelliJ IDEA
- Atom

I have used Floobits extensively, and it provided a really nice experience in the beginning. You feel like you are working on the same code, with very little lag, and you can discuss the same code while looking at it. However, after a while, I started feeling the pains of using this plugin. So, here are some pros and cons.

The following are the pros:

- Free
- Easy to start with and set up
- Live editing
- Follow pair
- Unfollow pair

The following are the cons:

- No shared terminal by default; you need to install Flooty.
- Very bad at syncing new files; I always needed to start and stop it several times.
- The code stays just on the one pair partner that is sharing their repository.
- Very few end-to-end security features.
- You need to make the code public on GitHub.

Alright – I hope you have chosen your favorite IDE for your favorite programming language. Now, we can go on to the next aspect of remote pair programming: setting up screen sharing, as a good addition to the whole remote pair programming experience.

Setting up screen sharing

While some people consider this optional, I really like to also see my pairing partner's screen. It's good that we already set up the IDE and that we can see the remote code, but some activities are done outside the IDE. You sometimes need to use a terminal window, browse through some files in your filesystem, or check an image to add it to your screen. All sorts of things need to be done outside the IDE. And while your pair partner is doing that, you just stay in the dark if you don't see their screen.

We have two categories of screen sharing tools:

- **Screen sharing and remote desktop**: The first category is screen sharing and remote desktop tools. These are great for seeing your remote pair partner's screen and being able to interact with it. But it uses more bandwidth than the option to share the screen just as video.

  Programming on a remote shared desktop for a long time is not an option for me. I just use this to see my pair partner's screen, and I use the IDE with a remote pair programming add-on to edit the code.

- **Screen sharing as video**: The second category is screen sharing as video. This is a simpler approach that consumes far less bandwidth than the previous option.

Here are some tools for screen sharing that are available now on the market. For each, you will see the pros and the cons so that you know if they fit your needs. There isn't a one-size-fits-all tool, so you either find one that fits your context like a glove, or you'll need to compromise. It's a good idea to try more tools before choosing the one that you think is the best for you.

Introducing TeamViewer

TeamViewer is a screen sharing and remote desktop software. It is probably the most well-known screen sharing tool and is available on multiple operating systems. I used to like it a lot. It used to be my go-to screen sharing tool, but during the last few years, updates made it buggier. I couldn't use it anymore. But it remains a good tool, with the condition that it connects and it works for you.

The following are the pros:

- Free for individuals
- Available on the main operating systems: macOS, Windows, Linux, iOS, and Android
- Smooth remote access and control
- Very good image quality

The following are the cons:

- The support for Linux has not been very good for the past few years; I would avoid it if I were a Linux user.
- It has good latency, but sometimes works very slowly.
- You need the app installed on both ends.

Next, let's see how to share our screens with the AnyDesk app.

Introducing AnyDesk

This is a screen sharing and remote desktop software. It is available on any operating system and it works well, is simple, and is fast. It has less lag than TeamViewer, and sometimes, it even feels like you are both on your computer. With good high-quality internet, it works well.

The following are the pros:

- Free for individuals
- Available on the main operating systems: macOS, Windows, Linux, iOS, Android, FreeBSD, Raspberry Pi, and Chrome OS
- Smooth remote access and control
- Good security and privacy
- Very good image quality
- Low latency
- Stable remote control, even at a long distance

The following are the cons:

- Not very well known.

- You need the app installed on both ends.

Next, we move to Screen.

Introducing Screen

Screen provides screen sharing and remote desktop capabilities. It works well, it's stable, and I know a few teams who have used it with great success. It definitely works better than TeamViewer, especially because it's stable and almost has no lag, and for me, it's a good alternative. AnyDesk or Screen are equally as useful for me in the context of remote pair programming.

The following are the pros:

- Free for individuals.

- Available on the main operating systems: macOS, Windows, Linux, iOS, and Android.

- Can be integrated with Slack.

- Good image quality.

- Low latency.

- Stable remote control.

- It was built with remote pair programming in mind.

- You can draw on top of the screen, to highlight areas.

- Contains video and audio, so no need for any other software.

- Can be integrated with Google Calendar for recurring meetings.

The following are the cons:

- Not well known.

- You need the app installed on both ends.

Next up is Use Together.

Introducing Use Together

This works with any editor, and it also works with any window that you choose to share with your pair partner, or with a group of people. It is a mix between a shared control tool and an audio-conferencing tool that is end-to-end encrypted. It's an interesting choice, but I would prefer having more features that focus on remote pair programming.

The following are the pros:

- Free for individuals.

- Easy to use.

- Low latency.

- Voice conferencing.

- End-to-end encryption.

- Live editing.

- You can share any window with a group and they can interact with it.

The following are the cons:

- It doesn't have the follow pair functionality.

After Use Together, we move to Tuple.

Introducing Tuple

This is a remote pair programming app that works with any editor, but it's dedicated to macOS. So, you cannot use it on other operating systems such as Windows or Linux. It's built for remote pair programming, as a reaction to the hole left in the market when Screen Hero was discontinued. It has video and audio embedded into the system, together with good remote and local control for two people. The software claims to have good security and privacy.

The following are the pros:

- Easy to set up

- Low latency

- Video conferencing

- Security

- Privacy

- Live editing
- Has **Single Sign-On (SSO)** for enterprises

The following are the cons:

- Subscription-based
- Available only on macOS

Next up is Zoom.

Introducing Zoom

This is a screen sharing and audio-video conferencing software. It probably provides the best image quality out there, can be stable for a long period of time, and has a high frame rate per second. It really is smooth and easy to use; the remote image is easy to watch.

The only downside of Zoom is that it has potential security and privacy issues that haven't been solved at the time of writing.

The following are the pros:

- Free for individuals
- Available on the main operating systems: macOS, Windows, Linux, iOS, and Android
- Easy to set up
- Low latency
- Video conferencing
- Audio conferencing
- Very stable HD image
- Very stable HD screen sharing image
- Good sound

The following are the cons:

- There have been a few security incidents in the past.
- Privacy is not its strong suit.

- More difficult to pair with a screen sharing as a video tool, as you aren't able to interact.

- Rotation becomes more difficult because of screen sharing as video, but mob.sh can help.

Next up, we have Google Meet.

Introducing Google Meet

This is a screen sharing and audio-video conferencing software. It's available for anyone who has a Google account. It's not the best video and audio-conferencing tool, but because of its wide availability, it's often the best option, as you don't need to set up another tool.

The following are the pros:

- Free for individuals

- Available on the main operating systems: macOS, Windows, Linux, iOS, and Android

- Easy to set up

- Highly available for any Google user

- Video conferencing

- Audio conferencing

- Screen sharing

The following are the cons:

- As it's a Google creation, the privacy aspect for it is not apparent.

- Can have high latency, especially for high-distance connections.

- The sound is good, but it can suffer on high-distance connections.

- It allows only HD – 720p, and even then, sometimes, it demotes the quality to 360p, without any obvious reason to.

- Screen sharing is the same as the image, only HD – 720p, and the quality is demoted to 360p without you being able to make any adjustments to it.

- More difficult to pair with a screen sharing video tool, as you aren't able to interact with it.

- Rotation becomes more difficult because of screen sharing as video, but mob.sh can help.

Next, we move to Skype.

Introducing Skype

Skype was a revolution some years back when we could suddenly have video calls with people around us. But in the meantime, its services have degraded, with the competition appearing strong due to their many enhancements. For me, Skype is not very stable, though I use it from time to time. I only use it for remote pair programming if it's the last option available.

The following are the pros:

- Free for individuals

- Available on the main operating systems: macOS, Windows, Linux, iOS, and Android

- Easy to set up

- Many people have an account

- Video conferencing

- Audio conferencing

- Screen sharing

The following are the cons:

- As it's owned by Microsoft, the privacy aspect for it is not apparent.

- Can have high latency, especially for high-distance connections.

- Sound is not great, and it can suffer especially on high-distance connections.

- More difficult to pair with a screen sharing video tool, as you aren't able to interact.

- Rotation becomes more difficult because of screen sharing as video, but mob.sh can help.

You should now have at least one good option for screen sharing, as a nice addition to the rest of the remote pair programming bundle. One more thing you need to know is how to use the source control well in a remote pair programming approach. There are a few guidelines that will make your life a lot easier, especially when you're remote pairing, but not only then. So, let's see more details about source control guidelines.

Learning to use source control

Let's look at some guidelines on how to use source control in a (remote) pair programming context. Some people might even enforce these guidelines and call them rules, making them part of the coding guidelines of the team. The most important thing is that the team understands why it's important to respect these guidelines.

Source control tools

Like any programmer, I have some favorite tools. Yours may be different, and that is fine. I want to explain why I use a distributed source control, and why I would never go back to centralized source control.

When I started programming, we were using these tools such as CVS, SVN, and Source Safe to manage code contributions. There were many teams who didn't have any source control, and I always found that scary. From the start, using Source Safe didn't feel safe at all. It would lose files and references, and it was never a reliable tool. CVS was complicated to use; you needed a lot of experience with the tool so that you didn't break it. SVN was said to be the better CVS, and that was true in most areas. It was still cumbersome to use, especially when solving conflicts. Sometimes, merging the result of a couple of days' worth of work would require 2 or 3 extra days to solve conflicts.

When you are a beginner programmer, you work slower than your experienced colleagues, and you don't commit every day as you should. Because of that, you have more conflicts. The rule of committing daily was a good practice, even though it was not enforced that well back in the day, at least where I was working.

When distributed source control came to the market, it was a big deal. The first such tool I used was Mercurial. Linus Torvalds was using it with the Linux kernel, and it sounded interesting. Mercurial is not a free tool, and it wasn't easily available if your organization didn't provide it.

Using Mercurial, compared to other source control tools, was such a relief. You could have your own branch to commit more often on. You could integrate your work with the work of others a lot easier. The conflict resolution was so much better than SVN. It was like a new era for source control tools.

After a while, Linus Torvalds decided to write his own tool for the Linux kernel. This is how Git appeared. Of course, as with Linux, Git was free to use by anyone. At that moment, the revolution started, when people were moving from the old source control tools to Git.

My preferred source control tool is now Git, for many reasons:

- Very easy to set up.

- Easy to start working with it; you just need to know 3-4 commands.

- It can work on any operating system.

- Branching is very easy.

- You are forced to write a commit message.

- Source control diff is very easy to use.

- You can easily integrate various diff tools.

- Conflict resolution is very simple.

- You don't need to wait for a source control server to start working (that was very annoying with SVN, especially with many programmers accessing the same server).

- You can work from anywhere, without even having access to the internet (SVN was very restrictive from that point of view).

- You can give your work to another colleague to review, without integrating it into the main branch (this is extremely useful for remote work, for junior programmers).

There are probably many other reasons to like a tool such as Git. The essence of a good source control tool for me is that it is distributed and not centralized; it shouldn't depend on a server.

However, there are a few things to keep in mind while working with Git. For starters, it is difficult to understand the whole branching mechanism. I remember that it took me a while to fully understand how complex branching can get, if you use it to its full power. Also, if you aren't used to using a command line and command-line commands with specific arguments and argument types, Git can become disconcerting. It is a steep learning curve if you want to become a power user. But you can get started with the basics, and then learn more and more over time. Nevertheless, the problem that any source control tool is solving is complex, and the solution cannot be simpler than the problem.

Now that you know my opinion on source control tools, let's put them into action. Before that, you will learn a few good practices regarding source control tool usage with remote pair programming.

Commit often

It's a good practice to commit often, regardless of whether you work solo or in a pair. Often, committing practices can be very different, depending on your skills, knowledge, programming language, coding environment, project, and many, many other aspects. So, I won't tell you to commit every 5 minutes in a local source control repository, because that would be too narrow minded, but I will give you some heuristics on how I commit as often as I can.

Here are the reasons for me to commit:

- Part of a feature is done.
- All the tests are written and green for a user scenario.
- I take a break in a stable state.
- The preparatory refactoring is done.
- One characterization test is done.
- One unit test is done.
- One unit test is green.
- The refactoring after adding a unit test is done.

The time I spend between commits is no longer than a few minutes. I try to commit maybe every 2 to 5 or 10 minutes at the latest, with a good average of 2-3 minutes when I'm working on a project I know. It might sound crazy to commit that often, but it's a weight off my mind to know that I always have an undo button. After committing that often, I usually pack the micro commits into a bigger commit and push it to the main branch, from my branch. By doing this, the micro commits are for me, and for my flow, but the big commit is for my team, and for any other programmer that might come after me.

Incremental thinking is the concept you need to use when committing often. It's not just about the safety, the flow state, and all the efficiency that comes with commits. You can't have any of that without thinking about the small increments that make you go from point A to point B. Refining knowledge, filtering it, and splitting it into pieces that are 2-10-minute commits is what you need to do.

Ensemble commits

Ensemble programming is the practice of developing with others, as opposed to solo programming. Pair programming is an approach to ensemble programming, but there is also mob programming. Why is the distinction important?

A commit in an ensemble programming context is different, because we can only make one commit, but the commit needs to contain a reference to all the programmers in the group. In a commit log, you will only see the alias and name of the committer. But it's important to acknowledge the contribution of both members in a pair, or all the members in a mob.

This is a commit message from one of my remote pairing sessions, where my partner is the committer and I'm the co-author:

```
commit d6a3b90e95b5e4f356c4236b55707a21465ca67e
Author: Harald Reingruber <undiscloded_email@email.email>
Date:    Thu May 28 09:05:15 2020 +0200

    Show correct start and endpoint names in the results page
header


Co-Authored-By: Adrian Bolboaca <undiscloded_email@email.email>
```

I really like this approach of showing who your partner in crime is in the body of the commit message because it shows a future contributor who changed the code. When we use pair programming, the committer is not the only person who affected changes on the code; the other pair partner had an impact as well. Unless we use these types of commit messages, that information might be lost. At the same time, this type of commit is an acknowledgment of the work the two people did together, rather than saying that only the committer worked, while the other pairing partner didn't do anything. Until we have a source control system that permits multiple committers for the same changeset, we are stuck with a solution like the one I presented in the previous example.

Rotation

A good tool for passing code when rotating is **mob.sh**. It is a tool that was made for mob programming, but it works the same with remote pair programming. Especially when you're remote pair programming with some tools, such as if you are screen sharing, you need to rotate fast. When you have a shared IDE, you don't need to use this type of tool for rotation, because everything is enabled by default. While mob.sh was made for fast rotation with local mob programming, I would also recommend using it for remote mob and remote pair programming. I am sure these commit guidelines will make your life a lot easier and better as a remote pair programmer. Use them well, while taking care of all the details I mentioned previously. Now, it's time to close this chapter with my favorite technical setup list.

Using two computers for coding and remote screening

It's nice to see the code in front of you and, at the same time, be able to see the person you are working with. The experience of remote pair programming becomes a lot warmer and nicer as you feel like your remote pair partner is closer to you. I think collaboration is a lot better when you have at least two screens.

Now that I've explained all the technical aspects of remote pair programming, here is my favorite setup for remote pair programming:

- Computer 1:

  a) Google Hangout/Zoom/Skype for video and audio

  b) Zoom for remote screen sharing

  c) External microphone with a tripod stand

  c) External USB sound card for the external microphone

  d) External webcam with tripod

  e) Headphones

- Computer 2:

  a) Code editor/IDE

  b) Remote pairing add-on such as Floobits/Code With Me

- Light:

  a) One lamp from the front, with a light diffuser

  b) One lamp for a backlight, from a lateral position, on the wall at the back of me

This is my favorite setup; you might feel the same as I do. Try it and see how it works for you. Regardless, the idea is that you need two displays: one to see your pair partner and another to see the code. Actually, the first display is like a remote digital presence of your pair partner, to enable our human nature – to feel like we are closer than we are.

Summary

In this chapter, we covered a perhaps unexpected crash course on audio and video, screen sharing, how to use an IDE that is appropriate for remote pair programming, and then a few guidelines about source control usage. We finished this chapter with a setup example for remote pair programming.

This was probably the most technical non-programming, non-coding chapter. Nevertheless, we need to take into account more than *let's sit and start writing some code*, because there are far more important aspects when it comes to remote pair programming. It might seem that coding is overshadowed by all these technical details, but that's not true. We need to get used to all these technical details, use them appropriately, and then start coding. You will feel like you had the best coding experience, and you won't want to stop working in this way.

We have our setup, and we can start remote pair programming. The next chapter will be about how to enhance your remote pair programming experience with pair programming-specific techniques and styles. We will look at the best ways to interact with various remote pairing partners, depending on your context, your knowledge and skills, their knowledge and skills, and the given problem or task that you need to solve. Good remote pair programming means adapting your techniques and styles to what you are doing, and that is what you will learn about in the next chapter.

Further reading

- *Data Privacy Concerns with Google*: `https://hackernoon.com/data-privacy-concerns-with-google-b946f2b7afea`

- *Data Breach*: `https://www.techadvisor.co.uk/feature/small-business/uks-most-infamous-data-breaches-3788338/`

- *Data Privacy and Current Architecture*: `https://hackernoon.com/data-privacy-why-the-existing-architecture-is-in-dire-need-of-evolution-or-part-1-2713n2h99`

6
Remote Pair Programming-Specific Techniques and Styles

Now that we are set up for remote pair programming, it's time to learn how to use some pair programming techniques and styles specifically for remote work. We will look at the technicalities of video, audio, screen sharing, and IDEs to the technicalities of remote pairing. We with then recap some of the main pair programming techniques and styles that you read about in *Chapter 3, Usual Pair Programming Techniques and Styles*. After that, we'll add a remote flavor on top of this so that you can use these techniques and styles with your colleagues.

In this chapter, we're going to cover the following main topics:

- Understanding general setup
- Understanding the remote driver-navigator technique
- Remote ping-pong technique

- Remote beginner-advanced technique
- Traditional pairing style
- Remote elastic pair programming style
- Remote strong style
- Good remote practices

Recap of main concepts of pair programming

When we're learning about something, we say that *repetition is the mother of learning*. So, let's repeat, in short, the main concepts of pair programming techniques and styles:

- The **driver** is the one writing the code and focuses on small details. Usually, the driver is in charge and makes all the decisions.

- The **navigator** observes the driver writing the code and focuses on long-term decisions. Also, the navigator suggests ideas, comes up with options, and shows the potential risks, dangers, or drawbacks of the current code.

- **Rotation** is the moment when the driver and the navigator change roles: the driver becomes the navigator and vice versa. Depending on the technique and style, it can happen more or less often, or it can even not happen at all.

- **Setup** refers to what you need to start your pair programming session: computer(s), an extra keyboard, a mouse, source control access, video, audio, screen sharing, an IDE, but also information about the knowledge of your partner; for example, if you need to be more like a trainer, like a student, or more like an equal partner.

The concepts of driver and navigator come from car racing, where you have two people: the driver is holding the wheel and all the commands of the car, while the navigator knows the terrain, map, dangers, and opportunities of the road. In racing, the navigator needs to assist the driver with sufficient but not too much information just ahead of an event. This allows the driver to adjust the controls according to the road conditions. The purpose is to be as fast as possible, but without risking going off the road, destroying the car, or injuring the crew.

With these concepts in mind, let's see what we need to do to have a good, healthy environment for remote pair programming. Let's look at some checklists that will help you ask good questions and make the appropriate decisions.

Understanding general setup

In *Chapter 5, Remote Pair Programming Setup*, you read about the options for setting up your environment for remote pair programming. But before you use any of the techniques we will talk about in this chapter, it is important to consider the following questions so that your pair programming session turns out to be a success.

The following are some questions to consider before setting up your environment:

1. What programming language (for example, C#, Rust, Java, C++)?
2. What library versions (for example, JDK 8 or .NET 5)?
3. What is the source control access?
4. Which tools do we use for video and audio (for example, Zoom or Google Meet)?
5. Which remote programming tools do we use (for example, CodeTogether or Floobits)?

Now, I want to remind you of my favorite remote pair programming setup. There are a few more aspects to this setup, all of which will be covered in the following checklists:

1. Install the **coding environment**:

   a). Install a specific Code Editor/IDE (IntelliJ IDEA or Visual Studio Code).

   b). Install a programming language.

   c). Install the libraries needed for the programming language.

   d). Install specific libraries needed by the solution from the source control repository.

2. Check the system for **audio or video**:

   a). The audio/video tool works (for example Zoom, Google Meet, or Skype).

   b). The screen sharing solution works (for example, TeamViewer or AnyDesk).

   c). Your microphone works and is compatible with the audio/video tool.

   d). Your headphones work.

   e). You are using the appropriate video camera.

   f). The image is centered on your face.

   g). The light is good; not too strong, not too dark.

   h). Uses cable internet.

3.   Check the system where you will perform **coding**:

a). Your coding editor works (for example IntelliJ IDEA or Visual Studio Code).

b). The remote pair programming tool works (for example CodeTogether or Floobits).

c). Uses cable internet

4.   Set up the **Environment**:

a). Make sure you have a pen and paper at hand.

b). A glass of water.

c). Close your windows to avoid disturbing sounds that your partner will hear louder than you.

This is the best setup I know, and it can be adapted to any of the techniques and styles that you will read about in more detail in the upcoming sections. In the next section, we will learn about the remote driver-navigator technique.

Understanding the remote driver-navigator technique

For the remote **driver-navigator** technique, you need, as the name suggests, a driver and a navigator, with the specific roles we explained at the beginning of this chapter. Using this technique, you don't rotate that much, or even at all. In this context, you do want to rotate, so both partners need to have access to the source control repository.

Let's learn how to use the remote driver-navigator technique in a remote context. These are all ideas, tips, and tricks that come from my own personal experience. I am sure any experienced remote pair programmer can add more of those, but in the following sections, you will find what I found to be essential.

Remote setup

Besides the general setup that you read about at the beginning of this chapter, there are some particularities for the remote driver-navigator.

You need to make sure you have *access to your source control repository (if you rotate)* before you start your remote pair programming session.

Remote specifics – driver

When you are the driver, you need to code, explain, express your intent in clear words, and ask for a second opinion from your navigator. Sometimes, the navigator will not seem too present, and will sometimes start asking questions or stating opinions that are different than your direction. Remember that it's the responsibility of the navigator to focus on high-level decisions such as design, architecture, and cross-functional concerns, and it's your responsibility to focus on the implementation details. Since you are remote, you don't really feel how close the navigator is to you and your work. Especially if there is a lot of silence, you might feel abandoned when you're coding. It's important to actively ask for opinions about the main steps you are taking. Take the time to ask questions to your navigator, especially in those moments when the decisions are not just implementation details, but are more high-level details, as described previously. With the driver-navigator pairing style, the driver is in charge of all the decisions. There are other ways of pairing, where the navigator would be in charge of the decision. But that doesn't mean you shouldn't use all the advice, wisdom, suggestions, and ideas that your navigator possesses to create fantastic code that both of you will be proud of in the future.

It's important to share both the screen and the code editor since the navigator needs to see everything that you are doing, even outside the IDE. You will often want to use a console, an emulator, a web browser, maybe search for a syntax, or learn how other people solve a specific problem. Usually, when the driver is stuck on an implementation detail (such as how to pass a reference from one context to another), the navigator typically activates and starts being the researcher. You will be able to see results or suggestions about how to do certain things using online or offline resources on their shared desktop.

You might get tired after a while when driving. You are focusing on very small details, and that can get tiring, especially if you are doing something new. Take a break as soon as you feel that you are starting to make mistakes. It's exactly these kinds of moments where you could try Pomodoro, or just take breaks. In *Chapter 4, Using Pair Programming in a Distributed System*, I recommended using Pomodoro (3 x 25-minute pairing sessions, with small breaks in-between, and a longer break at the end). Your brain gets tired faster than you think, and that is the moment when you start making mistakes. Sometimes, your partner will tell you: *I think it's time to take a break.* An experienced navigator can tell when you need a break. When you don't pair with an experienced navigator, it's important that you decide when to take breaks. Remote breaks are different, because you are both remote, and you need to synchronize. You can read more about remote breaks at the end of this chapter, in the *Good remote practices* section.

Remote specifics – navigator

When you are a navigator in this remote setup, you need to make sure you see everything the driver is doing, in good quality. You really need to have a shared screen as well, not just the shared code, as the driver could often go to an outside Terminal and test the app/ product in an emulator or web browser. That is why you should have two displays: one for the code and another for the shared screen. Otherwise, it becomes more difficult to manage.

The navigator is an active observer in this context. You may say just a few words every 10 minutes. However, if you need to, you can also be very active and try to steer the code, the code design, or the development in a certain direction.

You can become an advisor in this role of navigator, and when you see that something is not going in a clear direction, or you think you know that the direction is not good, you need to stop the driver and have a conversation. There are several ways of having this conversation:

- Express your opinion about how things should go forward.

- Ask for clarification so that you understand whether your perception of the current direction is correct.

- Ask coaching questions to make the driver understand the issue with the current direction.

- Ask the driver to stop, and then enter a design/architecture discussion with a remote whiteboard/remote diagram tool to enable a visual conversation.

The preceding list contains items that have been sorted by how difficulty. It's easier to state your opinion about a topic, but it's a lot harder to steer your conversation partner to the same conclusion through a chain of open questions. Furthermore, it is even more difficult to discuss something with a diagram/whiteboard tool without stating your opinion. Instead, you should start a discussion and reach an agreement about what is a good direction to take from this moment on.

The behaviors listed here demonstrate an increasing skill in pair programming and maybe also in technical coaching. However, as you begin to implement the actions further down the list, the more enjoyable the whole remote pair programming experience will be for everyone. Stating your opinion out loud without even validating your understanding about the coding direction typically results in conflict, especially in a remote environment. Even with all the video and audio tools that are available, we are still unable to grasp all the non-verbal aspects of communication from the other side. This limitation in human-to-human communication generates misunderstandings. Adding on top of that how us programmers tend to have very strong opinions, you already have the seeds for conflict. And usually, it's not a conflict of ideas, principles, or skills – it's just a conflict that's generated by remote miscommunication.

A good navigator will know how to swiftly state their opinion in small doses by adapting to their partner's opinion, asking clarifying questions step by step, trying to find the best common ground in-between the two, and guiding the driver to a good, high-level solution. Remember that the driver is responsible for the implementation details, while the navigator is responsible for the high-level solution: design, architecture, cross-functional concerns, and so on.

When you pair with the driver-navigator, it may feel silent. You may have moments when the driver seems to be doing all the work. In fact, the navigator is constantly reviewing the code that the driver writes, and if it's good, there's good progress, the partner is in a flow, and there is no need to stop. Often, I prefer noting down small recommendations, and when I've finished coding that small part, I come back with suggestions. A navigator that keeps interrupting the driver with cosmetic or simple improvements is not helping the partner at all.

Here is an example of some notes I take when I am a navigator:

- `General.cs 20`: Improve variable name.
- `General.cs 56`: Simplify function.
- `Config 34`: Use the same naming standard.
- `Soldier.cs 40`: Remove the else.
- `Soldier.cs 89`: Maybe extract to a different class.

Here, you can see that I am writing the filename, then the line number, and then the improvement suggestion that I have. After a Pomodoro (25 minutes), I might have *5-10* of these improvement ideas, and I want to see them discussed and incorporated quite fast, in a maximum of *2-3* hours after I have written them down. Our memory is selective, and I tend to write only the bare minimum on paper so that I can continue focusing on the coding part. That is why, when you're taking notes, it's important to act upon them as fast as possible, without breaking the flow; otherwise, you will forget your ideas.

Everybody has their own note-taking approaches, depending on how they feel and know their memory works. The preceding approach works for me, but feel free to adjust it for yourself. But please do take notes when you are a navigator.

Once you have mastered the remote driver-navigator, you can try remote ping-pong, an adaptation of this technique that can be really nice and useful to use in some circumstances. Let's see what it's all about.

Remote ping-pong technique

Ping-pong is a kind of driver-navigator where you rotate a lot. Specifically, this frequent rotation generates some issues, and remote ping-pong can be significantly more difficult in a remote setup due to the tools that we need to use.

The driver-navigator distinction remains, as in the technique explained previously, but their role changes very often. It's like having two hats that the two partners exchange very often. That is why the focus changes quite a lot from a driver who only focuses on short-term decisions and a navigator who focuses on long-term decisions, to both partners needing to focus on both aspects. This requires more experience in programming, software design, architecture, and the programming language that you use.

This approach is far more balanced than the driver-navigator one, and it requires that both programmers are experienced. You have more discussions about the future of the design as both partners envision some possible solutions, and those solutions need to be discussed and harmonized.

Ping-pong (remote) pair programming really shines when it's used together with **test-driven development (TDD)**. This is because the ping-pong technique fits really well with the steps and thinking behind TDD.

Let's learn how to create the setup for remote ping-pong and look at the specific expected behaviors for both the driver and the navigator.

Remote setup

Apart from the general setup, you need to define some rules that are specific to ping pong:

1. What flavor of ping-pong do we use (time-based or test-driven development)?
2. If it's time-based, what is the rotation interval?
3. If it's time-based, which tool do we use for the rotation interval (there are tools that show the same timer at both ends embedded in the IDE, as an IDE extension)?
4. How often should we take breaks (Pomodoro, every 45 minutes, or hourly)?
5. Choose the commit approach; you can read more at it the end of this chapter in the *Good remote practices* section.

The complexity of the setup comes from the frequent rotation that is required with this technique.

Remote specifics – driver

Everything from the driver-navigator technique applies to ping-pong as well, only the rotation is different. In driver-navigator, we don't rotate that often, whereas with ping-pong, we rotate very often.

The driver is not only focused on the implementation details, but also on understanding the long-term path. Since we are remote, things tend to evolve as you explain more, talk more, and show what you are doing in more detail in your code editor; this additional communication helps you overcome the disadvantages of remote audio and video communication. A driver in a remote ping-pong pair programming context is almost like a continuous code performer in front of an audience of 1. You need to be short, precise, clear, sufficiently abstract, but also efficient while coding.

Even for experienced programmers and experienced pair programmers, it's difficult to put this amount of energy into speaking and coding at the same time. For some, it results in more talking than coding while for others, it's just very tiring at the end of the day. This is the price you need to pay for remote ping pong pair programming. However, not everyone is like that. Some programmers get energy and satisfaction from driving by explaining what they do while driving.

Remote specifics – navigator

Everything from the driver-navigator technique applies to the ping-pong one as well, only the rotation is different. As we explained about the driver's role, the rotation during driver-navigations doesn't happen that often, while with ping-pong, we rotate very often.

The navigator is not only focused on long-term decisions, but also on looking at the implementation details that the current driver has chosen so that when the driver-navigator exchange their hats, the navigator can easily continue on the same path, along with the implementation details. Since you are remote, things change since you need to take more notes when your partner is driving, and you must always open a discussion on the long-term direction of the code.

As you may recall, I previously that I take notes during the sessions. With remote ping-pong, it becomes even more important to take notes about whatever is happening and what you would like to improve. Usually, when I become a driver, I have two choices: continue the train of thought of my partner and ignore the notes for now, or check the notes one by one and discuss any foreseen solutions with my partner. I choose to continue coding when I feel that we are in a flow and we need to figure out where we are going. However, don't take too long doing this and make sure that when you reach the next stable phase, you take your notes and start refactoring. Maybe this isn't that different in terms of a remote approach or a face-to-face approach, but still, you are not taking notes in front of your partner, and they don't really know if you have any suggestions. So, again, we lose a bit of communication with being remote. We need to overcompensate by being more structured and being more present in the pairing activities.

Remote ping-pong is a fun approach for me, and it's nice and effective for experienced programmers. Once you have mastered it, you might want to become a teacher, a mentor, or a technical coach, and the remote beginner-advanced technique is a very appropriate approach for such situations. We will look at this next.

Remote beginner-advanced technique

Beginner-advanced is like driver-navigator, but the driver is a beginner in programming and the navigator is an experienced programmer. This technique is about teaching a beginner in programming a specific technique such as committing often, using an **object-oriented programming** (**OOP**) language, or using a functional construct. There isn't much rotation with this technique, especially in the beginning. But when rotations start to happen, in a remote context, it might be very difficult for the beginner to know all the steps to be taken. Rotating will feel a lot more difficult when pairing remotely compared to pairing face to face.

Let's learn how to create the setup for the remote beginner-advanced technique and look at the specific expected behaviors for both the driver and the navigator.

Remote setup

Besides the general setup, the beginner needs to make sure everything is clear and works well. This typically means that before we start pairing, we need to have an initial session just with the remote desktop to make sure everything works. The experienced programmer gets through all the aspects of the remote pair programming checklist and explains to the beginner how everything should be and why. Consider this a lesson in remote pair programming, but before performing the actual programming together.

There is not much setup to do. However, the advanced programmer needs to be prepared to adjust the setup as the remote pair programming session progresses. The driver needs to be prepared to help whenever needed.

Remote specifics – driver

It can be awkward for the driver (the beginner) to be remote in an unfamiliar coding environment with a person who they may or may not know at all on the other side of the line. This is why the navigator's supports needs to be present on all sides: technical, environment, operational, theoretical, programming, and so on.

We have all been in unfamiliar situations where a teacher/mentor comes into the room to teach us. There's some emotion involved in this; nobody wants to feel stupid or look like a fool. These are all self-preservation instincts that come together with the evolution of human beings and are very normal. So, if you are a beginner, you need to know that it's normal to feel like that, but that it's also very normal to require a trainer that treats you with kindness and respect. We are remote, and it's sometimes difficult to feel what remote kindness and respect means, especially when we are starting out.

I've mentioned the Empty Cup story previously in this book. This is where you need to make room for new things to learn; you need to be open to learning. This aspect is essential to being a good beginner. It sounds funny, but as a trainer, I have often seen beginners who were almost trying to teach me what needs to be done. I am sure they did this because of their internal preservation instinct – to save themselves from being embarrassed. However, you should remember that we are pair programming to learn; otherwise, we wouldn't be here at all. Often, I have experienced more pushback from beginners than from advanced programmers, as the latter know there is always something to learn.

So, you need to be open, trust your partner, ask many (stupid or not) questions, open a debate when you have arguments, and try to understand what the other person is telling you before stating a final opinion.

Remote specifics – navigator

The beginner may not know programming at all, and as such, the navigator needs to take things very slowly when they're remote pairing. More importantly, the driver (the beginner) needs to use an environment that is somewhat familiar. The navigator needs to provide a lot of support and explain everything that is going on.

There is no such thing as a stupid question. For me, this is the motto that you need to keep in mind when pairing with a beginner. Any questions are allowed. Furthermore, when you're remote, it's difficult to understand how the beginner feels, their state of mind, how clear it is, what they are doing here, and so on. Because we are remote, the navigator needs to use the polling technique: they need to frequently ask the beginner if everything is good, if they have any questions, whether they feel they are on the same page, and more.

Training-wise, the navigator needs to use the basics of training: explain, do, recap, do some more, recap again. *Repetition is the mother of all learning* is well-suited to this context. More importantly, this is because we are remote and the navigator needs to repeat the aforementioned learning cycle several times.

There are recent studies that show that a beginner in programming will learn faster if they see a more experienced programmer write the code. This means that it is a good idea to switch from a navigator to a driver every once in a while. My approach is to use the show-and-tell method (coding live with deep explanations) for each topic. Then, we can switch roles, in that the beginner becomes the driver and tries to do the same. Sometimes, more exercises are involved, while other times, there is only one exercise.

Debriefing is compulsory when you're using beginner-advanced pairing, especially remotely. By having a final discussion on a specific topic, you can evaluate what the beginner has learned, what needs to be emphasized during a future pairing session, and the next important topics. The debriefing needs to be a calm, open, friendly discussion where honesty is encouraged. Debriefing remotely can be a bit more difficult than in person, though for some people, their shyness disappears, at least partially, because the other person is far away. Good HD video helps make the debriefing a lot better, nicer, and friendlier. The debriefing is usually the moment when you need good video, lightning, and sound the most from all the remote pair programming techniques.

At the end of any remote beginner-advanced pair programming session, it's important to ask your beginner what they liked about you, your approach, and what they feel would need improvement. You need to ask if you have helped them, and if so, in which way.

Beginner-advanced can be used at a large scale in an organization when you want to teach beginners how to program well. And if you are in a distributed, remote team by design, it's the way to go. Once you've used all these remote pair programming techniques, it's time to spice them up with some remote pair programming styles. Traditional style programming is how pairing starts naturally, so we'll cover its pluses and minuses in the next section.

Traditional pairing style

As we mentioned in *Chapter 3*, *Usual Pair Programming Techniques and Styles*, **traditional pairing** is like serendipity, where people with similar concepts, ideas, and values start working closer together as partners. You can see this in every software development team when one colleague asks another for help with some specific matter. It happens when the *helper* is knowledgeable about the topic and can provide clear speed-up for the development at hand.

By following this serendipity, some people start understanding that they like working closer to each other. That is the moment when you see them working together more often, sometimes on the same task.

Now, let's look at the setup for the traditional pairing style and the specific expected behaviors when we use this style in a remote approach.

Remote setup

For the traditional pairing style, there is nothing specific to set up in addition to the general setup we presented at the beginning of this chapter.

Remote specifics

This style suffers a few changes when we are in a distributed team. It's not that easy, or impossible if it's a fully distributed team, to see if your preferred colleague is at their desk and you can now ask to pair for a while. You need to compensate for the lack of this simple physical approach with the remote communication tools that the team has. Many teams use *Slack*, which has various communication channels. Here, you might have a *Pair with me* channel, where everyone who's interested in pairing is part of that channel and receives notifications from their colleagues in need of pairing. Other options are to always discuss, in a regular daily meeting, every person's planned activity for today, and then make sure that pairing is part of the conversation. Without these kinds of tools, you cannot have that serendipity to just make pairing happen like it does in a physical office.

Traditional pairing works well in a remote setup, but you start having these smaller groups of people pairing with each other. Issues appear when they only pair in-between themselves, inside these small groups of people. As we mentioned previously, when I first explained the traditional pairing style in *Chapter 3*, *Usual Pair Programming Techniques and Styles*, you start having these smaller groups of people who like pairing with each other. But this approach generates a split in coding standards, programming approaches, preferred solutions, and so on. When someone outside of this smaller group of people who like to pair together start working on the code, it will seem weird, difficult to understand, and hard to change. The end effect is that you lose time, and more defects will probably appear, which usually happens when we don't understand code that well. This problem – creating a split in the team – is even more common with remote, distributed work. Sometimes, it's not even visible until you start seeing the number of defects increase; that is, if someone is counting the number of defects and observing their progression. To fix this, you need some technical leadership to be put in place. It can be a formal team leader, an informal programming leader who is highly respected by anyone, a software architect, or any other solution in this direction.

Let me tell you a story about a distributed team that was having issues with the coding style. There were four JavaScript developers in four cross-functional teams, all working on the same code-base and the same product. Of the four developers, two were in Romania, one was in Canada, and one was in Argentina. Because of the time difference, even if the Romanian teams worked later, they only had a few hours of time in common.

The issues started appearing when we saw no progress on the JavaScript side after a while. There was a lot of tension between the Romanian leading developer and the Argentinian developer. The code that the Argentinian wrote yesterday was always changed, almost completely, by the Romanian developer the next day. When this happened, the Argentinian became angry and would change it back. It seemed at first like a silly, childish game, but it affected productivity. I started talking with both of them, and with the engineering manager by my side, I started remote pairing together. I framed it as an experiment to level their practices and come up with common coding and implementation standards.

At first, there was some resistance since the Romanian believed the Argentinian wasn't worth their time. Anyway, they started remote pairing 1 hour per day. After one sprint (they were using Scrum with 2-week sprints), they started getting along. We saw progress; there was no more re-rewriting the other person's rewritten code. After a few sprints, I saw both of them remote pairing when needed, not necessarily every day, but maybe once or twice per week. I have told you this story because it's a good example of how you can harmonize details of programming practices with remote pair programming by using the traditional remote pair programming style.

The traditional style is good for beginners. You start working together remotely, you make progress, you start learning, but you can feel that something is missing. After getting used to a person, it's good to experiment with some more dynamic approaches to pair programming. Remote elastic pair programming and the remote strong style fill this gap. Check them out, and use them when appropriate. They are tools, and it's important to use the right tool for the job.

Remote elastic pair programming style

As we discussed in *Chapter 3, Usual Pair Programming Techniques and Styles*, **elastic pair programming** is a style when any of the two partners can take the keyboard and become the driver. It is a style well-suited for experienced programmers who have trust in each other and can work smoothly together. Everything about elastic pair programming is based on consensus. It's probably the most pleasant way of working, but it is also probably the most difficult to achieve in a world where we programmers have strong opinions about everything.

Excellent communication, the ability to negotiate, to let go, to listen, and to choose the best solution no matter who came up with it are some of the essential skills for this style. It is a complete pleasure to work with people who have all these skills, and maybe more. Also, this style is a good example of visibly efficient pairing. Any programmer should strive to become proficient in elastic pair programming and use it when it is appropriate, depending on the context.

Let's learn how to create the setup for the remote elastic pair programming style, and what is specific when using this style remotely.

Remote setup

There is no additional setup for this technique on top of what you would normally do for driver-navigator.

Remote specifics

There are some barriers to using elastic pair programming remotely, especially because we need to switch often and fast, typically because you have an idea and want to share it. Programmers are highly impatient when they're working in an elastic style; it's that joy of knowing a good answer and wanting to share it fast. If the technology doesn't help you switch fast and show your solution in that moment, you can easily become frustrated and say remote pair programming doesn't work.

To overcome these barriers of fast switching, you need to have a good source control sharing option. You can read more about these options in the *Remote commit approach* section, later in this chapter. If I were to commit-push-pull every time I wanted to switch, that would be highly annoying. So, in this situation, tools such as *Floobits* or *CodeTogether* help a lot. Another option that is appropriate for almost all techniques and styles is to use a remote machine in the cloud where both partners join. In this way, both partners work in the same ecosystem, on the same IDE, and if there's no lag, everything is just great.

Debriefing is very important, especially in a remote setup. When using remote elastic pair programming, I tend to feel the need to debrief a lot more often than just at the end of the session. It's almost a rule inside my head that I want to make partial debriefs before each small break, so every 25 minutes, up to an hour. You are not in the same room with the other person, you don't know exactly if the current flow is appropriate, so what better way to find out than to ask sooner? Discuss all the different aspects, be open about everything, and you will feel like an old married couple that can discuss everything and anything without any taboos. The remote aspect pushes us into more conversations – especially, when we find ourselves coding in uncharted territory, such as a new programming language, library, business area, business domain, and so on. The more novelty there is, the more debriefing you need.

I want to repeat the importance of **ensemble commits**. Both partners work on the same piece of code, and it's essential that both are mentioned in the comments of the changeset from your source control repository. We touched on this previously, in *Chapter 5, Remote Pair Programming Setup*, in the *Ensemble commits* section, so please go back and quickly refresh on this topic before you start using remote elastic pair programming.

Visual and audio feel a lot more important with remote elastic pair programming because you communicate more. Compared to the traditional style or remote style, where the communication happens more from one side and less from the other, with remote elastic pair programming, you have a lot more communication from both sides. For me, it's essential to have good audio and video when working like this. I want to see my pair well when debriefing. I want to understand how my pairing partner feels, more than the words they are conveying. That is where good video and audio help a lot. I first found the name for this style of pairing from *Ferdinando Santacroce*, who was my partner in a few remote pair programming sessions that I recorded and posted for *codecasts* online. Even now, I remember pairing with *Nando*, as it was a very likable, fun, liberating coding experience. Even though we have never met before, it was our first interaction; all the movements were so nice, smooth, and natural. We were discussing a lot about what to do, but at any moment, one of us would try things out and immediately ask for feedback from the other. Nando had been using this style of pairing with his team for a while. All the team members were experienced programmers, and they knew how to get over their egos and be able to have discussions using technical arguments and choose the appropriate solutions. For these kinds of teams, you don't need many rules, techniques, styles, guidelines, processes, or any other form of overhead. You just need to trust them to get the job done, through real collaboration and openness based on their experience and thought process. This is how I would describe my pairing experience with Nando, when I found the name for this way of working together: **elastic pairing**.

So, elastic pairing is for experienced, social programmers who want to work well together in a real team where the team is a lot more than the sum of the parts. The next style is very different, and it comes from mob programming. It's different compared to any other style, and it has its use in specific contexts.

Remote strong style

As we discussed in *Chapter 3, Usual Pair Programming Techniques and Styles*, **strong style** is a very specific way of pairing that is used a lot in mob programming.

There is the driver, who writes the code and focuses on short-term minor details but cannot decide on anything. The driver only focuses on the low-level implementation details, which can be rectified by the navigator at any point in time. A good practice is for the driver to ask for confirmation from the navigator before starting to implement the navigator's idea. With strong style, you can say that the driver acts as a smart keyboard, who is just implementing the navigator's directions.

Then, there is the navigator, who makes all the decisions and focuses on the long-term strategy. The navigator is usually more experienced and carries out responsibilities from a strategic and structural point of view. The navigator thinks more about software design, the architecture, its impact on other features, the speed of development, solution complexity regarding the driver's knowledge, and so on.

You can say that strong style is the opposite of everything that we have discussed so far. Recall the driving analogy I provided at the beginning of this chapter. Even that analogy loses its meaning as now, the driver only holds the wheel in their hands, but the navigator can overwrite the commands at any time. The navigator can also be a kind of driver, by proxy, when needed. It might seem like an odd approach, and if you are very used to the techniques and style that we have discussed so far, you will probably feel like it's not a good idea. But it has its usefulness in some contexts. We need to remember that it comes from mob programming, where there is a group and the group needs to get along.

So, you need to be more like a smart and benevolent dictator to make sure the group stays productive, without entering many fruitless discussions. So, there you go, we have reached the context where remote strong style is also useful for pair programming: when you want to show an approach that would generate analysis-paralysis, rather than trying it out with code and then discussing it. When you have an idea of how to implement something but you don't know how to explain it, or it would be easier to show, then start pairing and be the navigator by dictating to the driver what to do.

But at this point, the following question arises: why don't you do that from the driver's position? There are a few answers to this question as well. First of all, you might not know the language that well, but you may be proficient in the following:

- Software design
- Test-driven development
- Refactoring
- Dealing with legacy code
- Software architecture
- Any other technology-agnostic tool

So, this style is appropriate for technical coaches, software architects (who hopefully still code and pair with people), team leaders, and so on. Secondly, you might have an idea of how to do things, but it would break your concentration to focus on the typing, software design direction, and explaining what you are doing. It seems like a lot to take in at the same time.

In the following sections, you will see that there is no specific remote setup, and we will dive a lot deeper into the remote specifics of remote strong style.

Remote setup

You don't need any specific setup for this technique.

Remote specifics

Communication is paramount when using remote strong style pairing. In a face-to-face setup, it's a lot easier to relate to the navigator and trying to understand what we are doing and why. In a remote context, all that non-verbal communication and drawing diagrams needs to be compensated by clear and efficient verbal communication. That is why the navigator needs a good-quality microphone and a very good audio setup.

Explanations need to be more precise and anchored into visual elements. Imagine that you are pairing with someone and you both have a screen in front of you. You can easily go to the screen and point to where you want the driver to do something. With remote strong style, that is not that natural and easy. Even if you have a cursor that you can show on the driver's screen, it takes longer, it breaks the flow, and I wouldn't recommend it. That is why I have provided some tricks I learned from *Llewellyn Falco* on how to express yourself quickly and efficiently when following a remote strong style approach. You need to speak with clear instructions, like the following (incomplete) set of examples:

- **State the line**: Line 10: Rename variable.

  When you're telling your driver what to do, you need to start with the line, and then with what to do.

- **New line**: Line 14.5: Add a for loop.

  This one seems a bit weird, but it's brilliant. It's shorter to say *14.5* than *insert a line after line 14*. It leads to better productivity, less communication bandwidth, and faster coding.

- **Exact command**: Highlight method name at line 45, extract method, or less abstract: Highlight the `computeSum` method at line 45, and then press *CTRL+ALT+M* to extract the method.

  The level of abstraction depends on the driver's skills with the IDE, programming language, and programming in general. It's preferable to communicate as abstractly as you can, but if your driver doesn't know the shortcut to extract a method, you need to spell it out, at least in the beginning.

- **Create file**: Click under the `Nova` namespace, add the `General.js` file.

- **Choose file**: Go to the `Gov.Special` namespace open the `PayAlgorithm.js` file.

There are probably many variations of instructions like the ones provided in this list, but I hope you got the idea that you need to communicate clearly and specifically.

The driver needs to do just one thing. That is the reason why you have these instructions. Maybe the navigator has many ideas and many variations of those ideas in their head, but the driver needs to know exactly what to do next, and when that's done, the next instruction needs to come from the navigator. When using strong style pairing, a navigator should not explain what they want to do at a high level of abstraction, and at the same time explain at a low level of implementation detail. This approach introduces confusion. We call this confusion a zoom-in for implementation details and a zoom-out for high-level abstractions. Rather, the navigator will give just one instruction, and after that chain of instructions is completed, we have a debrief, and we talk about what happened.

The navigator needs extremely good remote communication skills. The navigator speaks at the higher level of abstraction that is understood by the driver, but is careful not to speak above the level of understanding of the driver. For example, I might say *let's extract a strategy from those conditionals*, or I might need to explain this step by step; that is, *create an interface, create a method in the interface named like this, extract the first strategy into a new file and name it in this way, extract the second strategy, extract the third strategy*, and so on. This is a very simple example of two extremes talking in a very abstract way or very close to the ground.

The navigator needs to quickly adapt to the level of knowledge of the driver. If you are starting with a driver for the first time, during the first few minutes you are testing the water and adjusting to the driver's level of understanding. Of course, the driver learns as well, and after a while, you will be more and more abstract. An abstract language is preferable because the navigator can focus on the big picture, and overall, the pair is more productive.

In a remote context, communicating like this is paramount. When you are in a face-to-face context, you can still take a piece of paper and discuss everything with your partner. You can explain what a strategy pattern is, why we need it, and the alternatives; you can turn into a trainer for 15 minutes before going back to being a navigator. When you are remote, this type of training is more difficult, even with remote whiteboard tools. That is why the quality and level of communication from the navigator greatly impacts the overall experience of remote pair programming within strong style.

Trust your navigator. I need to stress the importance of trust in (remote) strong style pairing. This trust is more difficult to achieve when you are remote than when you are face to face. But if you are the driver, try to make an effort not to resist any of the ideas of the navigator. Try for an hour and see where you get. If you like it, you will want to continue further; otherwise, have a debrief with your navigator and state your ideas, opinions, and feelings about how things are going. If you are the navigator, it's important to tell the driver where you want to go. You also need to ask for trust when something weird happens: *I know this will be strange, but trust me for 5 minutes, and then we will talk about it.* Don't leave your driver completely in the dark, especially for longer periods of time. There needs to be some closure to, maybe weird, approaches. When remote, I think it's a good practice to have shorter work iterations, followed by debriefing periods. You need debriefs more often, not necessarily for longer.

Stop and have a dialogue when things become unclear. I have mentioned the importance of debriefing previously. Either of the partners should ask for a debriefing when things are unclear. The driver is mostly listening and doing what the navigator is doing. There is not much time to discuss or to ask deeper questions. So, that is why the debriefing is very important; otherwise, the driver might start getting frustrated easily about what we are doing here.

The level of detail in the debriefing depends a lot on the skill levels of both partners. With two experienced programmers, you will use very abstract concepts, with few words to encompass these complicated concepts. With one beginner and one experienced programmer, the experienced programmer needs to start being more like a trainer, and explain everything that happened at a low level of abstraction. Sometimes, this entails revisiting code or getting through other materials, such as books, blog posts, videos, and so on. Alternatively, the debriefing can be just about how we felt during the last pairing session. This allows us to have a short retrospective and adjust to the way things are going.

Recall when we talked about video quality in *Chapter 5, Remote Pair Programming Setup,* including the lightning in the room and on your face, the audio quality, and screen sharing. All these aspects become essential for a good, enjoyable debriefing for strong style pairing.

Now that you know how to use remote strong style pairing, it's time to practice it. Have a bit of patience with your partner in the beginning; it's not that easy to work like that for the first time – I know that from my personal experience. But before you start to pair, read some good remote practices that could apply to all the remote pair programming techniques and styles.

Good remote practices

Let's take a look at some good practices that apply to all the remote pair programming techniques and styles. You may find them basic, or you might feel surprised about some of them. I guess it depends on everyone's personal experience with pair programming, and with remote pair programming in particular.

Let's look at some recommended good remote practices that you should try using right away.

Remote breaks

Remote breaks are different than when you are pairing side by side with your partner, in front of the same monitor. When you are in the same room, you probably go out together, or go to the coffee machine, but you will still know when your partner is back. When you are remote, it's important to prepare some more. Here is how I prepare my remote breaks:

1. Before taking a break, agree on a specific break duration: *Let's take 5 minutes.*

2. When leaving your desk, explicitly say: *I am leaving now, you can still see my video, but I will mute my audio.*

3. When you're going back to your desk, explicitly say: *I am back, can you still see and hear me?*

It might seem like a basic ritual, but it does help to know that your partner is gone, has come back, the video connection is still going well, and so on.

Secondary communication channel

Sometimes, communications die. The internet doesn't work anymore, there's a power outage, the tool for video and audio communication is suffering a disconnection, and many other things like that. Because of that, it's important to establish a secondary communication channel before you even start to pair. Ideally, this second communication channel should be installed on another device other than your computer, such as on your phone.

I typically use *Slack* or *WhatsApp*, but it's your choice on which tool to use. Your remote partner may think you are late getting back from that break, and you might think the same, but in fact, it's a problem resulting from the audio-video tool. So, for example, if you see that your partner is taking longer breaks than initially agreed, use that secondary channel. Or, if you see that your remote partner has suddenly lost all connection, wait for a minute, and ask on that channel.

It did occur to me while working before that I needed to stop a remote pair programming session because of technical issues such as connections, the internet, power outages, and so on. It's important to know about these as soon as possible, and not lose any time waiting for your remote partner to come back when you could know they are not coming back.

Remote commit approach

Since we are pairing remotely, it's not an immediate thought to have the same commit repository that you would have when pairing face to face. We now have two computers that are connected via the internet, unlike in the face-to-face approach, where we have one computer with the code and another with the source control. So, we need to choose the remote commit approach:

> **Commit-push-pull**: Here, you are using a distributed source control system (such as Git or Mercurial) in a centralized approach (such as Subversion). But usually, you need a working branch to do that; you can only do this on the main branch in very small projects. You need to create a **short-lived** branch (I need to emphasize even more the short-lived part, meaning maximum a day) where both partners will push and pull the code as a communication environment. The advantage of this approach is that it's fast to use, easy to understand, and easy to start. The disadvantage is that you have a new branch that needs to be merged with the main branch, and you might lose time, or it might produce some merge hell in the meantime.
>
> I am always using this when it's my own pet project, and only me and my current partner are working on it. There's no risk since you are working on the main branch; there's no need to create a new branch and no need to merge. In other situations, you might want to consider other approaches, depending on how difficult or risky a merge would be in your context.

- **Shared repository**: Both partners are committing to the same repository, which sits on one of the computers. When using Floobits, for example, this is how things work. Only one partner commits for both partners.

> You can also share a folder remotely and open the code from the shared folder. Then, either only one partner commits, or you can get SSH access through a Terminal to commit remotely.

- **Code on a remote virtual machine**: This means that you set up a machine in the cloud with all the code, editors, source control, and so on, and both of the partners join in remotely.

  This is a good idea, especially when you're ensemble programming in bigger groups, such as with mob programming or when the setup is difficult to make because of the application's complexity (such as C++ embedded or Rust). This way, both partners are remote and share the same coding repository, without the need to sync anything and wait for a push or pull from the other side.

Choose wisely between these commit approaches, as each of them has pluses and minuses, and none of them are perfect. This is probably the most difficult change with respect to traditional, face-to-face programming.

Summary

We have come to the end of this chapter, where we saw how the previously discussed pair programming techniques and styles can be adapted to remote pair programming.

There are techniques and styles appropriate for experienced programmers, experienced beginner programmers, and those that are somewhere in-between the two. Reading about them is just the beginning; you need to get there and start experimenting with each. The order I placed these techniques in in this chapter was not random. I recommend that you start with the first technique, try it out, make it work for you, and then continue with the next one.

Your remote pair programming can be significantly better if you are conscious about the remote pair programming techniques and styles you are using. I hope you have learned how to use each, at least on a theoretical level, and can now start applying them at a practical level.

Programming becomes fun and productive when you're working remotely, so take your team on a journey to discover these remote pair programming techniques and styles. You will not feel bad for doing so.

In the next chapter, you will learn more about video and audio. We will get technical again and provide details on how to manipulate sound and video devices so that you can amazing quality streams. Don't worry – you don't need to be a sound engineer to understand this; we will just cover the fundamentals that will help you understand why you need to make certain choices when dealing with sound and video.

Section 3: Tools to Enhance Remote Pair Programming

This section shows how we can use appropriate tools to have a good, effective pair programming setup.

This section has the following chapters:

- *Chapter 7, Voice and Audio*
- *Chapter 8, Source Control*
- *Chapter 9, Remote Access*

7
Video and Audio

The topic of audio and video was partially covered in *Chapter 5, Remote Pair Programming Setup*. You may consider that the information provided there was enough, and quite technical. However, during this chapter, we will cover additional topics that will help you have great sound and video as they are highly essential for a seamless remote pairing experience. We will look at how professionals, such as actors and singers, use their voice and steal some good habits from them. We will also see how professional video and audio producers keep their sound and video simple and clean, which is a delight for any viewer or listener.

In this chapter, we're going to cover the following main topics:

- Recap of what we have learned so far
- Learning to enhance video
- Learning to enhance audio
- Enhancing speech

Recap of what we have learned so far

Let's look back at *Chapter 5, Remote Pair Programming Setup*, and list the main lessons about video and audio. We want to create a great virtual experience for our partner, which is why we want to put so much effort into all these technical details.

There are some general lessons that we can apply to both video and audio, and we will get into specific details of both of them.

General technical aspects

These are some general technical requirements that we talked about in *Chapter 5, Remote Pair Programming Setup*. It's worth mentioning that none of the items on this list are compulsory, but all of them are important for a great experience:

- Internet speed of at least 10 Mbit/s download and 5 Mbit/s upload.
- Use a wired internet connection.
- Use a room free of background noise.

The next aspect we will move on to is the comparison of audio and video.

Audio is more important than video

We also mentioned in *Chapter 5, Remote Pair Programming Setup*, that usually, audio is more important than video, because you are mostly talking about the code that you can see in front of you. Of course, without the code, you have nothing to talk about. But sharing a screen is something we are more used to than setting up good quality audio for our remote partner. That's why paying attention to audio is more important than paying attention to video. Furthermore, when you have bad audio for a few hours, you feel very tired, but when you have bad video, it's not that tiresome. Anyway, here is the distilled information for having great audio:

- Use a directional microphone.
- Position the microphone close to your mouth.
- Don't position the microphone too close as it will capture you breathing.
- Always use a headphone.
- Make sure the headset is comfortable for long time use; choose a studio headset.

Video settings

Good video brings another dimension to your virtual meeting. In *Chapter 5, Remote Pair Programming Setup*, we discussed how important non-verbal communication is to human beings. So, here is a list of the important settings that take your video connection from a good one to a great one:

- Have a stable video connection.
- Have an HD video camera or webcam.
- At least 24 **frames per second (FPS)**.
- Use frontal diffused light at all times.
- Use backlight for image depth.
- Position the camera on your face and shoulders.

Screen sharing settings

Screen sharing is something that we are more used to doing than optimizing audio and video settings. But still, there are some things to take into account when using screen sharing. Not all tools provide the same quality, or fidelity, so it's important to look for tools that are appropriate for the job. Here are the main things to take into account when screen sharing for remote pair programming:

- Share your screen in HD.
- Have at least two monitors – one for remote video and one for coding/shared screen purposes.
- Constantly share your screen, even when you have an IDE adapted for remote pairing.

Quality sound and video for the win

With great audio, video, and screen sharing, you will have a great virtual experience for remote pair programming. The key to having this experience is not necessarily paying a lot of money on professional equipment, but rather caring about your remote partner, and making the most out of what you already have. Here are a few things that don't cost anything, or don't cost a lot, but can make a huge difference:

- Learning how to position a microphone
- Testing your sound before starting

- Positioning your camera

- Using a cheap lamp to have appropriate lighting

- Testing your video before starting

- Asking for feedback on video and sound at the very start of your remote meeting

- Retrospecting on audio, video, screen sharing, IDEs, video conferencing tools, and other tools that you used for remote pairing at the end of each remote pair programming session

Now that we've looked back at *Chapter 5, Remote Pair Programming Setup*, let's add some more information on top. In the upcoming sections, we will deal with tweaks, plus some nice and useful additions to your video and audio setup. You may treat them as optional, but each will increase the quality of your pairing experience. All of them need some time to set up, learn, and get used to. After a while, you will feel that your pairing experience is a lot better, your remote partners will enjoy pairing with you, and you might even forget all the guidelines and rules provided, as they will become part of your daily habit.

Learning how to enhance video

This section is all about enhancing your video settings. In this section, you will learn about some ideas – call them tricks – for improving or enhancing your video quality. They are more like details that start to matter when you want to have really good quality. We will learn how looking into the camera becomes important and how, by using a green screen and virtual backgrounds, our video quality can be taken a notch higher.

Looking into the camera

I can tell you from my experience that looking into the camera is not at all a natural thing, and you need to practice a lot to get it right. It took me a few months to get used to the camera, even though I know other people who needed more like 1-2 years to get used to the camera. It's true – when we are talking about recording, or live training and coaching, it is a lot more intense, and a lot more difficult than remote pair programming. However, that doesn't mean that looking into the camera while remote pair programming is not difficult.

Looking the viewer in the eye is the catchphrase that you need to remember when you use a video camera. This approach will create a virtual connection with your partner because when they look at your image on their screen, it creates a natural approach. We humans prefer to be looked into each other's eyes when we're communicating; it's an attitude that inspires trust.

To be able to look the viewer in the eye, you need to look at their image as well. So, that means that the camera needs to be positioned very close to the monitor. Usually, my camera is positioned on top of the monitor that I use so that I can see my remote partner. In this way, when I look at that screen and at my partner, I look automatically into the camera.

Another situation arises when you have the second screen with the code base. Most of the time, you look at the code, so if your camera is on the other screen, which is positioned sideways, you're not looking your viewer in the eye. The only solution I see in this situation is to have the monitor with the image of your partner higher, with the camera on top of it, and the screen with the code immediately below that screen.

This setup is great, and I hope you have the space on your desk to make it work. It's something you only do once, when you create your working environment, and then you can forget about it. But it's one of those small things that really makes a difference.

Using a green screen

The green screen is something video producers have used for a long time. Why do we need it? It's useful when you want to have another background, other than your white, yellow, or painted wall behind you. It creates a nice experience, and you can be anywhere. If you feel like being on a tropical beach, you are there. It shows more than what you are saying; this background shows your current state of mind, which is also a part of non-verbal communication that we need to take into account. It's really a luxury item for remote pair programming, but it can be fun if you want to play with it.

You can find small green screens that cover the width of a desk or big green screens the size of a wall. Of course, we don't need to overdo it, as a small screen will suffice.

How does it work? You apply a visual effect called **chroma key**, which allows two images to be layered one on top of the other: your image and your wanted background. Chroma key is set to green, and it makes your background transparent, which allows you to layer the image with you on top of anything. You can use a still image, or you can use a video. It's magic – it's like the cinema! This chroma key can be applied to various live software tools. The tool I use the most is *OBS Studio*, which is a piece of open source software available for all the main operating systems. On top of OBS Studio, you use a virtual webcam that gets the video stream from OBS Studio and makes it visible, like a typical web camera, to any remote conferencing tool such as Zoom, Skype, Google Meet, and so on.

Many gamers use this green screen, especially when they want to show how they play. They have a green screen in the back, and they layer their image with the image of the game, in an area of the screen where it's not creating any visual discomfort. By doing this, you can see the game, while you also see the player talking and explaining what is going on.

> **Note**
>
> Be careful not to wear anything green, as you will become transparent in that area. As a rule, when using a green screen, you don't want to wear anything green or use any color that has green, as it might become partially transparent.

Using a virtual background

When you don't want to invest in a green screen, or you don't have a second computer to use its computing power for a chroma key, you can use the virtual background. Some video conferencing tools offer this option, usually as a premium paid feature, and you can discard your usual background while showing an image. It's more or less what a green screen does, but it's not performed by your software, such as OBS Studio, but directly by the remote conferencing tool.

It's a fun feature; it's good to have and easy to employ. However, it doesn't bring the same quality as a real green screen. It also comes with a cost, so if you pay for it for a few months, you could probably afford a real small green screen.

I would recommend that you try the virtual background first, and then start moving toward the more professional, better-quality option of a green screen. This transition is smoother, as you will need to learn a lot about light, effects, light positioning, and many other things that I will not get into now. I will leave you with the pleasure to discover all of these on your own.

The green screen and the virtual background started being more frequently used for meetings, or for remote pairing, during the 2020/2021 pandemic. Everyone needed to get out of their home in a way, as most people stayed in lockdown, at least for a few months. It's a nice way to get out of the office, while being at the office, or getting out of a usual, gray background, and showing that you are at a terrace in plain sun. Next, we will look at improving the audio quality while pair programming.

Learning to enhance audio

In this section, we will look at the techniques that can be used to enhance the quality of our audio. You will learn the correct way to speak into your microphone. After that, you will learn how to use an audio compressor to enhance your good microphone's sound, and how to use a pop filter, if you want to remove those annoying sounds when you breathe into the microphone. You will also learn how to perform the simplest and fastest soundcheck for when you start every remote pair programming session.

Speaking into the microphone

Have you ever had this issue where you are in a remote meeting and every few seconds, you hear someone breathing hard in your ear? Isn't that disturbing? Can you really focus when the volume is either too low or too high? No matter how much you keep adjusting the volume of your speakers, you will still be surprised about these variances. That is why you need to make sure you are not that person in the meeting, or in the remote pair programming team, that makes these disturbances for their partners.

First of all, you need to understand what the *correct distance from your microphone* is. Every microphone is different, and each needs to be a different distance from your mouth. Let's look at all the microphone types and understand how we need to use them:

- **Dynamic microphones**: These are cheap and versatile as they can be used for recording musical instruments, but also for voice. You need to keep a constant distance from these microphones and make sure you are not too close, as the sound will be distorted.

- **Large-diaphragm condenser microphones**: These are the best microphones for voice, though there are good dynamic microphones you can use for voice as well. You can speak closer to these microphones, and if you speak really close, like people on the radio do, it creates a bass effect. They really need an audio condenser, which we will look at in more detail later in this section.

- **Small-diaphragm condenser microphones**: These microphones are somewhere in-between the dynamic and the large diaphragm condenser microphones in the context of sound quality. You can speak into them at close range, as with the large-diaphragm condensers, but they won't yield the same professional sound as the large-diaphragm ones.

Secondly, you need to control your breathing. Never breathe into the microphone, always on top of the microphone. No matter which of the microphone types you have, you need to position it slightly below your mouth, and when you breathe, your breath should always go over the microphone, not directly onto it. I had this issue for a while with my condenser microphone, where I kept breathing into it. After 6 or so months, I started getting used to moving my head briefly on top of the microphone when I was breathing out. It's just a habit; you can get used to it. There is also another small tool that can help you, by stopping the air moving toward the microphone, called a **pop filter**. We will look at pop filters later in this section.

To conclude, the most important aspect is positioning the microphone, finding the correct distance from the microphone, and breathing out, over the top of the microphone.

Using an audio compressor

We briefly touched on the topic of audio compression in *Chapter 5, Remote Pair Programming Setup*. Now, it's time to look at this in more depth.

Technically, this is called **dynamic range compression**, and it means that while employing this effect, it will reduce the volume of loud sounds, while it will amplify quiet sounds. Why is this a good idea?

It's rather difficult to keep a constant speaking volume. For example, when you are excited about something, you might speak too loudly, which will have the effect of clipping the sound, and your remote partner won't hear anything anymore. On the other hand, there are some of us who speak in a really low voice, and the compressor will normalize the volume toward something that is easier to hear on the other side.

Also, another good usage is that it will reduce potential strong background noises, such as a dog barking out of the window, a strong siren from an ambulance passing, or anything like that. You might drop a pen or strike the microphone by mistake. These sounds can be really annoying, especially when you have your headphones on. The compressor will diminish the impact of these strong accidental sounds on the ears of your remote partner.

Another good use is that it lets you stay at a variable distance from the microphone. Especially with condenser microphones, you need to keep a relatively stable distance from the microphone as they aren't that sensitive. When we add the compressor to the equation, the captured sounds will be normalized, and you can keep a larger or smaller distance, while your remote partner will hear you perfectly well, at relatively the same volume.

Let's look at a technical detail. The following graph shows what a compressor does:

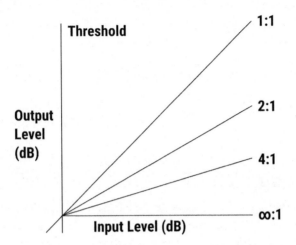

Figure 7.1 – Dynamic range audio compression graph

Here, you can see how the sound, over a volume threshold (represented in dB), will be diminished by a ratio you choose. You can set five parameters for a compressor:

- **Threshold value** (on the left of the graph): Only if you go over this value will the compression ratio will start being applied; if you stay under it, the volume will remain untouched.

    If you set a threshold of -10dB, anything over -10dB will be reduced by the compression ratio. A usual value for voice is -20dB.

- **Compression ratio** (on the right of the graph): The compression ratio is the amount by which your sound will be reduced in volume. If your initial sound is at 10dB and you apply a *1:4* ratio, your final sound will only get 2.5 dB louder. A usual value for voice is *1:4*.

- **Attack time**: This determines how quickly the compressor engages and reduces the volume of the audio. Its values are in milliseconds. A usual value for voice is 10 ms.

- **Release**: The release is the opposite of attack time. It determines how fast the compressor disengages and stops reducing the volume of the audio. Its values are again in milliseconds. A usual value for voice is around 40 ms.

- **Gain**: When we have reduced the volume by using the compressor, the overall volume will be too low. So, that is why, at the end, we need to add some gain. Usually, the gain is to compensate for everything that was lost through the compression rate. At the end, your sound should be at -10db, as a usual voice standard value for professional recording. So, add gain until your sound reaches -10db for a normal speaking tone, above the threshold value.

Yes, I know, we got very technical. Feel free to use this advice, especially if you made the effort to buy a professional microphone and sound card. It would be a pity to have them, but not utilize their real power.

Performing soundcheck

My habit is that before I start anything (remote pairing, video call, recording, and so on), I do a short soundcheck. I want to make sure that I don't waste someone else's time with my bad settings, or that I don't waste my time by recording something with bad sound that I need to rerecord it.

I hope you are all used to these kinds of checklists by now, so here is my soundcheck checklist:

- The microphone switch is on.
- The microphone levels show on the equalizer (either the software or the simple indicator from every conferencing software).
- Use a voice soundcheck phrase (check the list provided shortly).
- Make sure the sound volume is at -10dB and if not, increase microphone gain.
- The correct microphone is selected in the video conferencing tool.
- The correct speakers are selected in the video conferencing tool.

An important tip: when you're checking the microphone, don't blow or tap into it. You can use the typical *check 1, 2, 3*, or use one of the phrases that have been adapted for soundchecks, as they contain all the important sound categories that need to be checked. Here is a list of such phrases:

- The small pup gnawed a hole in the sock.
- Who is this pet? Say, he is wet. You never yet met a pet, I bet, as wet as they let this wet pet get.
- The fish twisted and turned on the bent hook.

- The beige hue on the waters of the loch impressed all, including the French queen, before she heard that symphony again, just as young Arthur wanted.

- The beauty of the view stunned the young boy.

I must confess I find all these phrases funny. I don't know the origin of these phrases; some of them might be quotes from some novels, but I know they are really good for voice soundchecks.

Why is a phrase better? Because you can see your volume not going over the normal -10dB value in a few seconds. You can check that your levels are good and that you are ready to continue.

Monitoring the sound

Sometimes, during your day, some settings may change. Quite often, remote conferencing tools will change some levels on your computer by themselves. It might happen that your sound is either too low or too high and it starts getting distorted. That is why it's a good idea to monitor the sound during the day. It's not like you are recording with an artist in a studio, but you should keep an eye on the settings to make sure your remote partner gets the sound quality they deserve.

There are various ways you can monitor your sound:

- **Hearing yourself while you are talking**: I wouldn't ever recommend this. It's weird. It's like you are drunk and cannot speak too fast. It's a common rookie mistake to do that, and then you find yourself in the situation where you cannot work very fast because you can hear yourself. This is an option only for very experienced podcasters, not for anyone else.

- **Observing virtual audio mixer levels**: This is the typical approach and is when you have a virtual mixer or volume indicator (even the one from the remote conferencing tool). The best virtual mixer, for this simple activity, will also show you the level of sound in dB, to make sure you are at that recommended -10dB value at all times.

- Observing physical audio mixer levels: This is more like the semi-professional, or even professional, approach. You will be able to see many things on that mixer, but I am afraid this might be too much just for remote pairing.

Monitoring your sound levels is a useful activity, and after you get used to it, it becomes second nature.

Adding a pop filter

A pop filter is a mesh that prevents air popping into the microphone, while still leaving the sound to go through.

This device typically attaches to the tripod of the microphone. Some professional microphones have a pop filter included inside it, so check your microphone's technical details. This option is usually good for singing, when there is a strong air flow from when the singer exhales in front of the microphone. It works really well for speaking, but it can be annoying to use when you're sitting, as it may move around, stop you from seeing the screen, and so on.

Also, you can use a foam pop filter, which is a round, spongy piece of foam that can be attached to the head of the microphone. Its size depends on the size of your microphone, so make sure that you check your microphone's size before ordering such a pop filter. This foam option is not as effective as the first one, but it's very good for speaking. While the first one is more for singing and making loud noises, this second one is more for speaking in a usual tone of voice.

Now that we've looked at how to improve and enhance audio, it's time to look at a more TV anchor topic: how to speak so that your remote pairing partner will understand you quickly, easily, and without more effort than needed.

Enhancing speech

Over the years, I have learned that you need more than good technical skills to get your message across. This is valid for both in-person and remote scenarios, which is why we will learn how to enhance speech. Even though the ideas presented in this section are essential for news anchors and radio presenters, you should get to know them if you want to have a good remote pairing experience, and you want to avoid throat ache at the end of the day.

In this section, you will learn how to employ diction to emphasize some words or phrases so that your message is received a lot better by your audience. Nobody wants to hear a low-tone, flat phrase as your message will sound very unappealing in a short period of time. And on top of that, you need to use words that are powerful and meaningful. A good speaker will use concise and clear sentences. To make all that happen, you also need to warm up your voice so that you sound nice and crispy. Let's look at all these techniques in detail.

Employing diction

Diction means that you choose a style to enunciate while speaking to make yourself very well understood. It's a complex topic: when to breathe, the tone you should use to start a phrase, how to continue using that phrase, which words get to be accentuated from the phrase, your talking speed, and many other aspects. I'm not an expert on this, but I really enjoy speaking with someone who uses appropriate diction.

Diction is something you can start working on now and keep mastering for the rest of your life, with the purpose of talking very clearly to your audience.

I think diction will not only help you in remote pairing but in any circumstance where you need to speak with people. Communication becomes easier, with less effort.

Choosing words

When you're talking with someone, vocabulary is very important. From my experience of public speaking, remote meetings, remote training sessions, remote coaching, and remote pair programming, I can say that I prefer not to use words that are difficult to understand, especially when remote.

Usually, I don't speak with native English speakers, so I try to use simple words that everybody is used to. Even though I sometimes feel the urge to use a more appropriate word, it may not be a very familiar term, so I refrain from using it. So, using simple words, from a simple vocabulary, is my approach.

Another aspect that I consider when choosing words is that I prefer not using words that are difficult to pronounce for me, or difficult to understand for my audience. I guess those words are very different for all of us. The important thing is to identify which words are clear, and where you get asked *sorry, what did you say?* Being asked that question means that you should stop using that word or phrase. That's my simple heuristic.

Warming up your voice

You might be surprised at how many times I found myself having a rough voice toward the end of the day, after teaching or pairing a few hours in a remote setting. I find it even more important to warm up my voice when talking remotely, because when you feel that your remote interlocutors aren't hearing you well enough, the natural reflex is to speak louder than you should, leading to throatache.

If you want to keep your voice going, and you care for your health, it's good to warm up your voice (especially in the winter), before you start pairing. You need a maximum of 5 minutes for that. And you can do this while you are starting up your computer, sound checking, and doing other activities.

I'm not an expert on this; you should read about this more or approach a professional singer or actor if you want to learn about this properly, but here is a checklist of what I know you need to do:

- Warm up your body.
- Loosen your head and face muscles.
- Take long deep breaths.
- Perform diaphragm exercises.
- Perform lip exercises.

It's a good idea to have *hot tea* (especially in the winter) or some *eucalyptus*-based candy because they help your throat a lot while speaking.

Summary

In this chapter, we covered some extras for video, audio, and speaking in a remote context. These ideas will help you in any remote situation, and most of them will even help your in-person work. I can tell you that I have learned these from many smart people and great presenters during my life, and using each of them adds one more drop of professionalism to any person's life.

Throughout this chapter, you learned how to improve your video by looking your audience in the eye, using backgrounds to change the scenery, and also how to use your voice in an efficient way. You looked at how to keep an appropriate distance from your microphone, how to perform a soundcheck, and how to stop delivering strong, unwanted sounds on the other side of the line. You then learned how important it is to warm up your voice, as well as how to use the appropriate vocabulary and your voice so that you can have a nice, simple conversation with your partner.

The next chapter will provide a detailed approach to source control usage with remote pair programming. We touched on that topic in *Chapter 5, Remote Pair Programming Setup*, and now it's time to understand the fundamentals of efficient source control usage that leads to best practices for remote pair programming.

8
Source Control Rules

Source control is an essential mechanism for remote pair programming, and it's for this reason that it deserves a dedicated chapter. After discussing source control rules in *Chapter 5, Remote Pair Programming Setup*, it's time to explain those rules. Sure—it's good to have rules, guidelines, and good practices, but it's also very important to understand the reasons behind having those rules. And as I have never seen in my life a rule without exceptions, it's also important to know the underlying necessity of that rule so that you know when to bend or disregard it. Of course, a rule remains a rule and a guideline remains a guideline, therefore they shouldn't be overtaken by their exceptions.

After a short recap of all the rules and guidelines that we have gone through during this book, we will get to explanations for each one of them. If you are an experienced programmer, pair programmer, or remote pair programmer, you will find this chapter particularly interesting. You know that the rules from *Chapter 5, Remote Pair Programming Setup,* provide efficiency, but there are situations in which we need to use reason and do things differently, and this chapter provides more complex thoughts on how to adapt our practices by using heuristics.

In this chapter, we're going to cover the following main topics:

- Recap of the source control rules
- Improving source control usage
- Using the commit types
- Understanding commit heuristics

Recap of the source control rules

In *Chapter 5, Remote Pair Programming Setup*, we discussed source control rules and all the essential information needed to start working as a remote pair. Now, it's time to recap on the rules we went through, and in the following sections we will elaborate on how to adapt them when the context requires it.

Using source control

Source control has become an essential part of the software development environment. Every programmer should use it well and with efficiency. Nevertheless, our source control usage depends a lot on our past experience, those who had the time and knowledge to teach us about it in the past, and the teams we have worked with and their practices. Approaches to source control differ from team to team, and there are various ideas and techniques. You learned about the following rules—or rather, guidelines—in *Chapter 5, Remote Pair Programming Setup*:

- Commit often
- Do ensemble commits
- Practice source control rotation

While committing often is almost always a good idea, you need to make sure your final commit to the main branch makes sense to your colleagues. The many—and small—commits are for your personal usage, to make sure you don't break the code and that you remember what you have done. At the end of any task, you need to take your broom, clean the room, clean your tools, and remove the dust from the final piece. With commits, the best approach is to merge those many small—or very small—commits into a large one that explains your full task, for the benefit of your colleagues. Your branch can remain parallel to other branches, if you need a detailed history of what you have done.

Committing often is a known practice, but ensemble commits and source control rotation are likely something new for a programmer who hasn't done remote pair programming yet. This first practice helps a remote pair programmer to understand who was working on that code. The second practice is a hack to help you change the code when switching driver and navigator, if you don't have specialized tools that enable seamless remote pair programming.

These techniques are great to start with, but there is a lot more to take into account when dealing with source control. You will be able to read further good advice on how to improve your source control usage while remote pair programming in the rest of this chapter.

Improving source control usage

There is more to source control than using good commits or having ensemble commits. Bad usage of source control is amplified when pairing remotely, thus it's even more important to respect some best practices.

Here is a list of the best practices I use for source control, which may already be familiar to you, in the form of a checklist:

- Use source control in any situation, no matter how small the project is.
- Add all resources to the source control (code, libraries, scripts, configuration, and so on).
- Check that your source control repository is functional before starting the project.
- Review the changeset before committing/pushing.
- Make sure newly added libraries are in the changeset as well.
- Only commit files that have meaningful changes (not non-behavioral changes such as spacing, alignment, styling, and so on).
- Use clear—ideally standardized—commit messages (start from the Linux kernel conventions).
- Ignore autogenerated files by compilers, analysis tools, and so on (for example, the /bin folder).
- Ignore **integrated development environment (IDE)** autogenerated files.

- When creating a branch, make it live for as short a time as possible (a few days maximum), then merge it back with the main branch. The branch needs to have a short life because otherwise it would diverge too much from the parent, and there would be more conflicts to resolve. The shorter the life of the branch, the fewer conflicts you have.

- Give good names to branches—ideally, use standard branch naming conventions

- When having multiple micro-commits (every few minutes), pack them into one bigger commit, and use the commit message guidelines mentioned in the *Using source control* section.

- Use the commit types for clarity and structure of the commits, to result in the following:

    a. A new feature

    b. Solved defects

    c. Improved code without behavior change = refactoring or styling or alignment

    d. Improved code design with behavior change = redesigning or rearchitecting

Let's see in more detail how my recommended commit types help, as they bring a lot of focus to your work. This type of focus is especially important with remote pair programming; however, it is also very important when doing solo work.

Using the commit types

The commit types were part of the previous checklist for best source control practices. We need to elaborate on these commit types as follows, and see how they can help you with each of the preceding scenarios:

- **New feature**: I found it useful to have a focus factor, and since I am always using a clear list of prioritized features that remain important for the next few days, it was evident that changesets need to relate to that feature. That's why whatever change I do (config file, database, adding a library, changing an **application programming interface (API)**, adding a code file, changing existing code, and so on) needs to be related to the feature I am working on. It's easy for me and my team to grasp changes when it's clear that a commit matches a particular feature as shown here:

```
commit d6a3b90e95b5e4f356c4236b55707a21465ca67z
Author: Adrian Bolboacă <adi@email.email>
Date:    Thu May 28 09:05:15 2020 +0200
```

```
    New feature: AB12324. Added the main part of
the feature; it still needs visual, cosmetic and UX
improvements. We can test it as a first version, and come
with improvements afterwards.
```

- **Solving a defect**: Another clear reason for changing the code is to fix a defect. You need to have a clear distinction between changing the code for fixing that defect and making other changes that involve style, structure, code clarification, or cosmetic changes. You should limit your code changes for this type of changeset because fixing a defect typically generates other defects. That is why the changes made to fix that defect need to be clear, in a small changeset, and marked as a defect fix. Often before fixing a defect, you almost always need to make the code better and clearer, and you need to remove clutter in the code to be able to fix the defect. You need to make those types of changes before bug fixing, and then mark them as code improvements. It's very important to note whether those code improvements are with or without behavior changes. This is illustrated in the following code snippet:

```
commit d6a3b90e95b5e4f356c4236b55707a21465ca67t

Author: Adrian Bolboacă adi@email.email>

Date:    Thu May 28 09:05:15 2020 +0200


    Solved defect: AB99238. The correct name of the start
point is now shown in the search results page.
```

- **Improving code**: It's a common approach that before adding any feature or fixing any defect, you *make room* for the change. I translate this concept of *making room* into two possible options for improving the code: without behavior changes (or refactoring), or with behavior changes. Code improvement without behavior changes is also called **safe refactoring**, and you can read more about that in specialized books on refactoring. Safe refactoring means that when you perform an operation in that order and in that context, no behavior changes can happen and no defects can be introduced. Safe refactoring is opposed to code improvements that will introduce behavior changes, even the smallest ones.

So, here, we have improved code without behavior changes = refactoring or styling or alignment:

```
commit d6a3b90e95b5e4f356c4236b55707a21465ca67n

Author: Adrian Bolboacă <adi@email.email>

Date:    Thu May 28 09:05:15 2020 +0200


    Preparatory refactoring before fixing defect AB99238.
```

> Improved the names inside the classes Result, Search and Point. Now the bug fix is clear.

Here, we have improved code design with behavior changes = redesigning or rearchitecting:

```
commit d6a3b90e95b5e4f356c4236b55707a21465ca671
Author: Adrian Bolboacă <adi@email.email>
Date:   Thu May 28 09:05:15 2020 +0200
```

In the previous code snippet, I improved the design before adding the AB12324 feature, to make room for the new change. I changed the design of Map, together with its tests, as the behavior needed to be changed together with the new feature. Now, work on the new feature can begin.

- **Changing code in a safe way**: J. B. Rainsberger often tells this story about changing code in a safe way. He was working on a web system, and he saw some inappropriate names for some text labels, on a page in the system. He started changing the names from label1 and label2 to more meaningful ones. After compiling the system, there was a big crash. Apparently, the name of the label was connected directly to a key in the database, and the key was the name of the label1 label. So, an apparently safe refactoring was shockingly unsafe. The lesson is: really make sure your safe refactorings don't introduce behavior changes. The main tool for that is a good battery of automated tests, on all levels: unit, component, integration, end to end.

Nevertheless, it's important to make a big distinction between the two types of code-improvement actions: without behavior changes and with behavior changes. Before fixing a defect or adding a feature, you should start with safe refactorings. These let you learn about the system and understand it better; you give better names to all the code artifacts; and it's easier for you to start making more substantial changes.

> **Never mix commit types in the same changeset**
>
> I find this essential for an organized way of working; it's crucial for a healthy state of mind. In this way, I always focus on all of the three working modes: new feature, solve defect, and improve code (in two ways: without behavior changes and with behavior changes).

As you can see, each commit message contains the commit type, an ID for the issue-tracking system (a board on the wall, or an electronic system), and a short comment about the changes that were performed on the code.

It's time to get into more details about commit heuristics, and explain the heuristics concept better.

Understanding commit heuristics

In *Chapter 5, Remote Pair Programming Setup*, I listed some of the heuristics I use for committing to source control. Let's first define what a heuristic is.

A **heuristic** is an approach to solving a problem by means of a method that might lead to a result, and that result is not necessarily optimal or ideal. Heuristics are useful where we cannot find a rational, best solution, and we rely more on observable traits of the system that, together with our past experience, generate one or more decisions. Heuristics are faster than rational, logical, provable (even mathematically probable) solutions, but don't always lead to a result. A heuristic is a shortcut to decision making; if you have taken that decision in the past in the same context, you will take the same decision now.

In knowledge work, we often take these types of shortcuts and decide based on previous experiences. The good side of heuristics is that you can take decisions really quickly, and most often the decisions solve the given problem. The bad side is that you never know if it's the best solution, because you instinctively attack the problem with your current knowledge and skills.

Heuristics are strongly related to our biases, and our biases come from our professional, personal, and social experience. Rebecca Wirfs-Brock discusses the importance of cultivating and growing our own heuristics, and understanding the boundaries of each heuristic. Also, it's important to self-analyze in retrospect after taking a decision based on heuristics, looking at how much it was based on your current biases and trying to identify those biases.

All of this introductory information is important because I want you to read about the following heuristics, taking into account that I have biases, as does any other person. Some of them are known biases, while others are not known biases. Your biases might be different, and that is why you might not appreciate my source control commit heuristics. Our experiences, environments, and focus might be different, and that is a big part of the differences in our biases. But even if you don't agree with my heuristics, try to formulate your heuristics, and try to identify as much as you can the biases on which you formulate your heuristics.

Let's discuss each of my commit heuristics. Each one of them influences the way in which I commit to the source control repository. I need you to understand that these commits are all performed on a local, personal, work branch.

Committing when part of a feature is done

I don't need a whole feature to be complete before committing. It's enough to have something done, even if it's very small, and to have a stable code base. The smallest increment I want to have done needs to be very small, but big enough to be able to receive feedback on it. This can be technical feedback (coding, design, architecture, security, and so on) or product design (user experience, user interface, solving users' needs, and so on).

Committing when all the tests are written, and green, for a user scenario

My confidence increases more and more as I keep adding tests for the new feature or for the existing system that I am working on. As my confidence increases I am more likely to commit, as I know the changeset makes sense, works, and solves the customer's problem. When all the tests are green (and of course, you almost always forget a test, but that's why we have review and feedback), it's a good time to make a commit. That doesn't mean this is the only moment I commit. There may have been tens of intermediary commits up to this point. Maybe I need 1 or 2 days to get there, so this is definitely not the first time I've made a commit. However, it's the first moment I know for sure I can get feedback from the product team, because if all my tests are green, this means I can assume all the aspects of the feature are implemented.

Committing before taking a break, in a stable state

I don't like taking breaks without having the code in a clear state. It bugs me as I cannot get my mind off the code, and that's not a real break when you keep thinking about your code and about your work. That simply means you are still working, but not at your desk.

Maybe you are like me—maybe you aren't, and you can stop your brain from working. As I know from behavioral psychology, our brain puts a topic in a closed drawer when we reach a type of closure on that topic. Otherwise, it will keep using background processing power to keep this topic alive.

Committing will put the topic into the drawer and will free my **random-access memory (RAM)**, thus making my break from work more enjoyable and making me more energetic for new challenges.

Committing when the preparatory refactoring is done

In the *Using the commit types* section of this chapter, we discussed the difference between code improvements that change behavior and code improvements that don't change behavior. The preparatory refactorings can be of both these types. A preparatory refactoring is also called *making room for a change*; it may be for a new feature or to fix a defect.

Most often when working with existing code, we don't have the code ready for the change we need. This situation is normal if the code intended to do just one simple operation. Now, we want to make it more complex, and we need to add some code to it. But before rushing into adding that new operation, we need to make sure the new code will find its place. It's like tidying up your wardrobe, before putting in the new clothes you have just bought. Or, it's like checking the route from your **Global Positioning System (GPS)**, making sure that the suggested route is not through a rough dirt road that might destroy your car. These checks, changes, and adaptations to the preliminary context are preparatory refactorings.

In my mind, these preparatory refactorings are separate from analyzing existing code or adding the new feature (or fixing the defect). You should make *only safe changes* to the existing code as preparatory refactorings. Think of it like tidying up your wardrobe, making room for new clothes, but if you don't get the new clothes, you can still use your wardrobe. Even more, you can use it better—and faster—because it's tidy. Only when I have finished tidying up my code can I start adding the new feature (or fix the defect).

On my route to the point where I can start adding the new feature or fix the defect, I need to use one or more preparatory refactorings. After each one of them, I like to make a commit, considering of course that all my tests are green and that everything works well without any defects or regressions.

Committing when one characterization test is done

This one is specific to working on existing code. Michael Feathers says the following:

Characterization tests are a different type of test than any other test. They refer to the moment when we write them, and they are independent from their type, scope, or running style (for example, end-to-end tests, unit tests, component tests, and so on). A characterization test is written after the code was written, and we want to characterize its behavior with tests. They are like a post-production documentation, and they help us understand how the system works, supplying a very necessary safety net for the coming changes. Of course, we write characterization tests when there aren't any, or an insufficient number of, tests for that code. Quite frequently it's the case that we don't have any automated tests at all for the existing code we are working on.

As mentioned before, a characterization test can be a big, end-to-end test, or it can focus only on a small behavior from a class. Still, it will characterize the system, in a larger or smaller scope. Writing a characterization test can be extremely time-consuming. This happened to me when I spent around 1 week on a first characterization test, but after that, everything started rolling better and better. There are many reasons why characterization tests can take so long: convoluted code; dependency graphs that are too complex; hard-to-understand code, or just the plain old spaghetti code that nobody understands, not even the initial team.

When we are dealing with existing code, when we need to change legacy code we first of all need to make sure we have a battery of tests that ensures our changes will not introduce defects or regressions. One way of achieving this is by writing tests that characterize the existing system. This is why Michael Feathers named them *characterization tests*.

These tests are different from the tests we write for a new feature because with a new feature we start from a hypothesis, start writing the test, and then implement the code for that test. Characterization tests don't start with a hypothesis, but rather with concrete code that works.

One characterization test (especially the first) takes a long time to write—anything from a few hours to a few days. It all depends on how unnecessarily complex the code is and how we can imagine a solution around this accidental complexity. You probably won't be able to respect the guideline of committing at the end of each day, especially when you write the first set of characterization tests. That's probably one of the few exceptions to that rule.

In any case, when you reach the end of that test you will be thrilled that it works, and you need to commit. Remember to take time to look at all the changes, and make sure there aren't any code improvements that change the behavior, because you don't yet have a safety net to tell you that you have changed the existing behavior.

Committing when one unit test is green

A unit test is first of all written, implemented, and then refactored, together with the production code that made it green. Whenever your test is green, it's time to commit. Of course, the testing code will not be great; it might be full of duplication and unnecessary coupling. But the focus was to make it green. You have reached this second goal (the first goal was to write it), and now it's time to commit.

A really, really good reason to commit now is that you want to perform refactoring as the next step. Sometimes, it has happened with me that while refactoring I made some changes that I thought were safe refactorings, but in fact I made the test go red. The best thing to do is to have an **Undo** button, and your safe, clear, simple **Undo** button is used to revert to the previous commit. This is the best reason to commit when on green, and not in the next step of refactoring after green.

Committing the refactoring after a unit test is a natural step after the previous step. When my focus is to make the test green, I don't want to write the best code. First of all, we need to admit that everything we write for the first time is not that good; it's even bad code. We need to look at it at least three times in order to make it good enough to commit. I am using here my mantra **first make it work, then make it better**.

Refactoring means improving the code without changing it's behavior. My changes are mostly about names for files, classes, functions, methods, variables, constants, namespaces, and so on. But they can also be about structure as I want to have similar structure in my code, because in this way I have a form that is easier to understand by me in the future, or by my colleagues.

After all these changes, I need to commit with a good, clear commit message. I typically prefer splitting my refactoring commits into more types, detailed as follows:

- Improved naming
- Improved structure (for example, my file has, in order, the following: namespace, imports, constants, variables, constructors , public methods, private methods)
- Cosmetic changes (the same number of tabs; remove empty lines; appropriate alignment; and so on)

Now, it's time to let you know my (known) biases on which the previous list of heuristics is based, as follows:

- Always try to write a test before writing the code. If you don't succeed, write a test after.
- Take very small steps so that you can free your mind from the current activity, and finalize the step with a commit.
- Working on existing code, assume this is as interesting as—if not even more interesting than—working on new code.
- Always start with preparatory refactorings to unclutter the code, before starting the structural refactoring.

- Write as many unit tests, in isolation, as you need in order to minimize the risk of defects and maximize the power of the safety net for future development.

- Take breaks every hour or so, and do something completely different from sitting in front of a computer (take a walk, eat an apple, discuss a book, call your plumber, and so on).

- Work on end-to-end features.

- Always split the features into small enough parts that stability is reached in around 1 hour.

- Use the mantra: make it work, then make it better; never make it perfect.

- There is no real pressure in delivering bad-quality code; my professional duty is to deliver the best code I can with my current skills and knowledge, and that includes tests.

- When doing something completely new, discuss with someone else your options and design ideas, and let it sit for a few days. When the problem is really complex, discuss it with as many diverse specialists as possible.

These are my heuristics, but as I mentioned before, it's important to identify your own. And, next time you discuss with someone how to do remote pair programming, start with exposing your heuristics and biases. Only after that can you have an effective, useful discussion based on facts.

Our experiences may be very different, and two radically different—or even opposite—points of view can both be valid; only the context is different. Identifying and presenting your own heuristics helps explain the context in which you live, and hence puts remote-pair-programming practices into a more specific context.

Summary

This chapter was a short but deep dive into source control usage for remote pair programming. After a brief recap of the guidelines for source control that you read about in *Chapter 5, Remote Pair Programming Setup*, we added a few guidelines upon which the initial guidelines are in fact based. After that, we saw a possibly new concept of commit types and explained how this can be extremely useful to you and your team.

Structuring your commits by commit types is a great way to spend less time wondering what happened with the code in the past. Toward the end of this chapter, we dealt with commit heuristics and with my known biases on which my heuristics are based. Clarifying and making transparent your heuristics and biases is a great way to have essential conversations about best practices with your remote pair programming partners, team members, colleagues, and friends.

The next, and last, chapter will be about working remotely and remote access. We have discussed this topic briefly in *Chapter 5, Remote Pair Programming Setup*; however, it's now time to get into more details. You will learn how to have a great remote experience while remote pair programming.

Further reading

- Additional information on `Commit` message conventions can be found at `https://git.wiki.kernel.org/index.php/CommitMessageConventions`.

- **R Rebecca Wirfs-Brock and Alex Bolboaca** – Design Challenges: OOP, Design Patterns, Heuristics at `https://mozaicworks.com/blog/rebecca-wirfs-brock-alex-bolboaca-design-challenges-oop-design-patterns-heuristics`.

- **Michael Feathers** – Characterization Testing at `https://michaelfeathers.silvrback.com/characterization-testing`.

9
Remote Access

Having reached the final chapter of the book, I hope I have helped to make this an enjoyable and useful read. We now have one final topic to discuss – remote access. We briefly discussed this topic in *Chapter 5, Remote Pair Programming Setup*, where you learned about the following topics:

- Setting up screen sharing
- Screen sharing and remote desktops
- Tools for remote desktops and screen sharing

In this chapter, we will go into more detail, as the topic requires some necessary additional information. That is why, during this chapter, we're going to cover the following main topics:

- Recapping the rules of remote pairing
- Understanding how remote access tools work
- Relying on tools
- Security for remote access

Recapping the rules of remote pairing

In *Chapter 5*, *Remote Pair Programming Setup*, we discussed the importance of remote access. Now it's time to recap the rules we went through. We require a tool for remote access, and it should have the following ideal features:

- It is free for individuals.

- It is available on all of the major operating systems, including both desktop and mobile applications.

- It is easy to install and set up.

- It offers smooth remote access and control.

- It offers good security and privacy.

- It has low latency (although this depends a lot on both partners' internet connections).

- It has very good image quality (minimum HD).

- It has stable remote control, even when used at long distances.

There are many tools on the market for remote access; sometimes, even video conferencing tools have remote access capabilities. Creating remote access software is not at all easy, especially across different operating systems – it becomes a real challenge. That is why such a tool needs a lot of attention from the software creator along with many, many updates to stay in line with the newest changes from the operating systems.

Let's explore, in more detail, what my main tools for remote access are and how I use them. Note that this is not a complete list of tools that are available on the market; rather, it is my experience and history with remote access tools over time. I am sure you also have your own experience of working with such tools since we tend to discuss far too much about which tool is better rather than the basic principles that a tool should respect.

Understanding how remote access tools work

In my experience, the video conferencing tools with remote access are not that great for remote access. And, I guess, I wrote the reason for this in the preceding paragraph. Remote access requires a lot of attention to many specific details and a ton of continuous testing with an operating system's changes, and if you just add remote access as an extra to a video conferencing tool, you will treat it as an extra entity.

Lag is a big issue when talking about remote access. All the video conferencing tools with remote access features that I have used so far have issues with lag. This is great if you want a fast pairing session of only 10 minutes. However, after a while, the lag becomes annoying, tiring, and you start wishing for a better tool to use. Lag is the killer of any good remote pair programming experience. That is the reason why I prefer pairing in a code editor with an add-on that permits remote pairing: the lag is almost gone, and you can remote pair as though your pairing partner is sitting near you.

Because of lag issues, I would never recommend that you use any video conferencing tools for remote pairing. You can use a dedicated remote access tool if you have a good internet connection and good computers at both ends. A remote access tool will use a lot more processing power and memory, and, usually, you need a better graphics card. If you don't have all these, then I would recommend you try the code editor with the add-on for remote pairing. So, it's up to you; there are many available options. Test them, try them, and see which of them is more appropriate for you.

In *Chapter 5, Remote Pair Programming Setup*, we presented some of the tools that work well for remote pair programming: TeamViewer, AnyDesk, and Screen. However, there is another option that we didn't cover, and that is Chrome Remote Desktop. This option comes in handy because it's attached to the popular web browser that many people already have installed, so it's easier to start using straight away.

I won't repeat myself in this chapter; instead, I will give you my unbiased, personal opinion about these tools. Throughout the book, I have tried to shake all my biases and be objective. In the following section, you will discover how I use these tools and a few stories about them.

TeamViewer

I learned about this tool a few years before it came onto the market. It was my favorite tool, and, for a long time, there weren't many alternatives. Back then, I was using Microsoft Windows, and it was great to access a remote desktop in no time. I was using it to help friends and family with different settings on their computers at a distance. Let's say that I was a kind of a designated system administrator. As I was traveling a lot, it proved to be very useful and easy to use.

At one point, TeamViewer began having more and more performance issues, and I seriously started questioning its reliability. It crashed more often and made it difficult to connect to remote computers. Even now, it has an issue with the lack of backward compatibility. This means that you always need to have the same version of the tool in order to make it work.

After switching to Linux, TeamViewer started becoming more and more difficult to use. Either it didn't connect, or it wasn't working. You could not select, click, or do anything on the remote desktop.

Remote pairing was good for a while with TeamViewer (that is, at the beginning) since it was the only tool that I knew of that could work across different operating systems. Of course, I was using the remote desktop from Microsoft Windows; however, for connecting with other operating systems, there weren't many options available. That was the moment when I started looking for new tools, and I found AnyDesk.

AnyDesk

After the issues I encountered using TeamViewer on Linux, along with its multiple performance issues, I started using AnyDesk. This feels similar to TeamViewer, and it was really easy to switch. Even now, I consider it as one of the best remote access tools. It has less lag than TeamViewer or any other tools I have used, so far, that support remote access across different operating systems.

At this point in time, I find it reliable, easy to use, and I would recommend anyone trying it. Of course, remote pair programming on a remote desktop is not the greatest thing for the long term, and I wouldn't recommend it for long-term usage with remote pair programming. However, I have found AnyDesk to be surprisingly efficient even for remote pair programming, along with its ability to make me feel like I am working on my local desktop instead.

Screen

As mentioned earlier in this chapter, I like having alternative tools because I am sure tools will crash at some point and stop working, and you always need a backup. This is where Screen comes onto the scene. I use it as a backup tool, not very often, but it proves to be useful when AnyDesk stops functioning.

It's not very often that AnyDesk stops functioning, but I find it reassuring that I have a second tool that I can use. It's not that Screen is worse than AnyDesk, it's just that I have used, out of habit, AnyDesk a lot more; it's just a personal choice.

Chrome Remote Desktop

Not everyone wants to install a tool for remote pair programming, especially if you have a short session. This is where Chrome Remote Desktop comes in handy. Many of my remote pair programming partners already have Google Chrome installed, so it's easy to start this remote desktop functionality. It does have many of the critical features, although it doesn't excel at reducing lag time.

Sometimes, the tool that is closest to your hand is the best. You shouldn't impose on your remote pairing partner to install different tools when you can use something they already have, and then start working. However, for a future session, you both can prepare with a better tool. Continuous improvement is the key, and don't aim for the best from the very beginning.

Your tool of choice

Nowadays, there are many tools for remote access. However, I don't want to discuss all of them and write detailed reviews. My purpose, in this book, is not to evaluate all the remote access tools that are out there. Tools keep appearing and disappearing from the market, and it's important that you choose the best for you.

Please don't consider the preceding list as a definitive one to use, but view it more like a guideline on how to use a remote access tool. I believe that an experience report on my tools and how I use them is more valuable than a dry tool review that doesn't say much about the use or the accurate needs for the remote access tools.

Certainly, I don't want to start a tool debate, as I find these types of debates to have little value. All tools are good for a given context and usage, and there is no point in describing any tool in absolute terms. This description of tools is only based on my experience and within my context.

The most important thing for me is to always have alternative options and to be flexible about the tools that I use. I have worked with suboptimal remote access tools many times because I wanted to focus on getting something done, or teaching or learning something. I prefer working with what's at hand rather than using all that time to make my environment perfect for me. I recommend that you also be flexible, and focus on the main aspects: be productive, learn, and teach something new.

Following this description of how I use remote access tools, let's examine how reliable they are. It's really important to understand how reliable our tools are and what we can do to maximize their reliability.

Relying on tools

I don't trust tools. My friends and colleagues know that I'm often saying that *Technology doesn't work*. You might feel the same, or you might be more optimistic. For me, the more I have worked in software development, the more I don't trust tools, as I know they will fail at any moment. It's a given for me.

The only thing I have left, after passing through the usual states of frustration, acceptance, and resignation is to acknowledge that I need to have a second plan for any tool so that my work is not destroyed by the malfunction of the tool.

When talking about remote access, I tend to prefer a tool, but I always have another one as a backup. It has happened, on numerous occasions, that we started remote pairing on a tool and it stopped working in the middle of the session. Then, we agreed to immediately use the second backup tool. So, there you go. Here is the first suggestion I have for you:

Have a second backup remote access tool available.

The same thing has also happened to me while pairing with video conferencing tools and even with video cameras. For one reason or another, they stopped working. A second video conferencing tool was always available and already installed. And I always had a webcam that should work if my primary camera didn't want to function anymore.

For code editors, it is more complicated to have a backup tool. However, at the very least, you can always use a simple, basic text editor, or a terminal editor, when your complex code editor crashes. Here is my second suggestion regarding tool reliability:

Learn how to use a simple text editor when your code editor crashes.

On one occasion, my code editor stopped working entirely, but I had a second one already installed. It only took a few minutes to start using that one. The key is that you already have an alternative installed and that you know how to use it well.

Bug magnet

Even when I started working as a programmer, all the bugs were sticking to me, in the same way a magnet attracts needles. My colleagues were always amazed when I would tell them stories about how systems had crashed on my computer or on computers I was using. After a period of profound frustration, I started liking it and considered that this bug magnet thing was a positive feature.

Throughout this book, I have told you about the advantages of remote access with code editor add-ons, as this makes you have almost no lag, and you feel like you are pairing with your remote partner near to you. However, I did have numerous issues with all of the add-ons that I used. All of them had bugs or strange defects that would hinder us from being as productive as we wanted. I have yet to see a remote access tool that is perfect or, at the very least, one that functions well in my presence.

Of course, you might be luckier than me and not be a bug magnet. However, if you are like me, try to hang in there. Resist the temptation of considering that remote pair programming is too difficult because nothing works. You can learn to fiddle with these less-than-perfect tools, and you can see how beautiful and rewarding remote pair programming is even if it's challenging at times.

Security for remote access

Perhaps one of the things that programmers don't consider strongly enough when it comes to remote pair programming is security. I would say that there are two types of security, as follows:

- **Personal security**: This includes following the best practices for cybersecurity.
- **Technical security**: Make sure you respect security guidelines.

Let's understand each of these in the following sections.

Personal security

When talking to security experts, one of the main focuses is on how an individual can make small mistakes that generate holes in the security of a software or hardware system. The most danger comes from how careful we are with our systems, considering that we know how our systems work and what could go wrong.

We might think that most errors come from the technical side and that our systems might have technical problems. However, most problems come from how we, the users, interact with the system, and how we create these holes without even knowing. There are many examples of security breaches based on strong passwords that were too complicated to be remembered, so they were written on a piece of paper and stuck onto the monitor. Or, where we have used the same password for all of our accounts, so when one is breached, many of the others can potentially be breached within minutes or hours.

Personal security is also about trust. We need to trust the person we are handing the control of our machine to. Throughout this book, I often recommended remote pairing with team members but also remote pairing with strangers, because there are so many things to learn. However, bear in mind that not all strangers might have good intentions. Be cautious and don't grant automatic access to anyone just because you are excited about a certain remote pair programming session. I'm not saying that you shouldn't trust people; it's just that you shouldn't be gullible, and make sure that you take precautions with people you don't know.

Within security, there is the **Principle of Least Privilege**, which says that you should assign to a new account (or to a person you barely know in our remote pair programming scenario) the fewest privileges possible, and then escalate privileges only when necessary. For instance, let's say that you need to grant access to a code repository. Don't directly grant administrator's rights to a person you barely know. A committer's role is enough, and all the commits can be evaluated by you or by someone else. If everything goes well, you can escalate these privileges, and grant a superior role when the commit evaluation is no longer necessary. The same goes for a remote access account. Don't give default all-time and all-around access to someone you pair with. In fact, I wouldn't give such a password to anyone, no matter how much I pair with them. The access rights only need to be for a small part of your system, with a limited period that expires by default. It's a lot easier to grant the same rights again – especially with a new remote pairing partner that you don't know that well – than to leave some access rights and forget that you even gave them.

Personal security is tricky because it involves taking a balanced approach between being open to people and using efficient tools and also being very vigilant about anything that might happen with a person, tool, or system we use. If we are extremely open to people, we might have issues after giving too much trust. If we are extremely paranoid, then we won't do anything anymore, and we will lose any opportunity to learn from other experienced people who won't do any harm. Balance is the key but with a constant eye on the possible risks and threats.

Technical security

When you leave a door open to access your computer, make sure you know what you are doing – particularly if you work with code that is not public, for an organization that handles delicate information, or if you work in a regulated environment. Of course, I imagine there are security experts in your organization as well. However, the tightest security is kept when all users of the system understand the risks and threats and act accordingly.

Here is a checklist of items to take into account when leaving a door open for remote access to your computer:

- Always use a password for remote access.
- Use strong passwords – ideally, generate them using a tool that checks their quality.
- Update your remote access software as soon as you are prompted to.
- Use a firewall, and learn how to use it well.
- Keep a log of remote access, and check it periodically.
- Always personally accept the people who have remote access.
- Remove the remote access grant at the end of each day for all your users.
- Use **Secure Shell (SSH)** when the tool permits.
- Use a VPN as much as possible.

This checklist is probably not complete or final, but it's what I have learned for now and what has served me well in the past. I recommend that you start using it, but also complement it with other ideas from your own experience, depending on your needs and your context.

There are many things to read regarding cybersecurity. The field is increasing at a rapid rate as systems become more and more connected and attacks start becoming more and more complex. In the *Further reading* section, at the end of this chapter, you will find a few references to public information that you should look into.

Summary

In this final chapter, we discussed how to make remote access both enjoyable and reliable for your remote pair programming sessions.

While a remote access tool needs to have certain characteristics to make our lives easier and to enable almost seamless remote work, it also needs to have certain security features that keep us safe from harm. It's not just about the tools that we use for remote access but also about all the tools that we use for remote pair programming. All our tools need to have a high-security performance, and we need to continuously audit them and improve their security as much as possible.

Remote access, in one way or another (just the code, or desktop sharing), is essential for remote pair programming. However, opening your desktop and your code on a remote communication tunnel is a risk that we need to take into account. Learn about how your tools and systems work, what the possible risks and threats are, and treat them with diligence and responsibility.

This was a great ride through the world of pair programming and remote work. The future of work is very different than what we have experienced so far. I am sure this book is a new brick for your learning on how to work efficiently in a distributed, remote environment, and it will bring you enormous benefits in your future work.

Have fun pairing!

Further reading

- Threat modeling methods: STRIVE, OCTAVE, CVSS, and more. Refer to this link, `https://resources.sei.cmu.edu/asset_files/WhitePaper/2018_019_001_524597.pdf`.

- The newest security threats can be found at `https://owasp.org`.

Packt>

Other Books You May Enjoy

If you enjoyed this book, you may be interested in these other books by Packt:

Supercharge your Slack Productivity

David Markovich

ISBN: 978-1-80056-962-1

- Understand how to set up a Slack workspace
- Migrate existing workspaces to your organization
- Explore expert tips and techniques for using Slack effectively
- Improve collaboration within your team by integrating multiple apps with Slack
- Find the right bots and apps to use for your workspace
- Discover how to build your own Slack bot
- Explore the right channels on Slack to improve your presence in professional communities
- Find the best solutions for automating your work directly through Slack

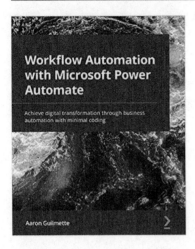

Workflow Automation with Microsoft Power Automate

Aaron Guilmette

ISBN: 978-1-83921-379-3

- Get to grips with the building blocks of Power Automate, its services, and core capabilities
- Explore connectors in Power Automate to automate email workflows
- Discover how to create a flow for copying files between two cloud services
- Understand the business process, connectors, and actions for creating approval flows
- Use flows to save responses submitted to a database through Microsoft Forms
- Find out how to integrate Power Automate with Microsoft Teams

Packt is searching for authors like you

If you're interested in becoming an author for Packt, please visit `authors.packtpub.com` and apply today. We have worked with thousands of developers and tech professionals, just like you, to help them share their insight with the global tech community. You can make a general application, apply for a specific hot topic that we are recruiting an author for, or submit your own idea.

Leave a review - let other readers know what you think

Please share your thoughts on this book with others by leaving a review on the site that you bought it from. If you purchased the book from Amazon, please leave us an honest review on this book's Amazon page. This is vital so that other potential readers can see and use your unbiased opinion to make purchasing decisions, we can understand what our customers think about our products, and our authors can see your feedback on the title that they have worked with Packt to create. It will only take a few minutes of your time, but is valuable to other potential customers, our authors, and Packt. Thank you!

Index

A

aggressive communication 73
AnyDesk
  about 135, 204
  advantages 135
  disadvantages 136
application programming
    interface (API) 190
assertive communication 73
audio
  about 122
  directional 122
  enhancing 179
  omnidirectional 122
  versus video 174
audio compressor, parameters
  attack time 181
  compression ratio 181
  gain 182
  release 181
  threshold value 181
audio enhancement
  microphone 179, 180
  pop filter, adding 184
  soundcheck, performing 182, 183
  sound, monitoring 183
  with audio compressor 180-182

B

Beginner-Advanced technique
  about 53
  advantages 54
  disadvantages 54
  remarks 55
  rotation 54
  setup 54
  usage scenario 54
Beginner-Beginner technique
  about 55
  advantages 56
  disadvantages 56
  remarks 57
  rotation 55
  setup 55
  usage scenario 56
bug magnet 206

C

cardioid pattern 122
characterization test 196
chroma key 177
Chrome Remote Desktop 205
CLion 131
code review 14
CodeTogether plugin
  about 130, 132
  advantages 132
  disadvantages 133
Code with me plugin 131
commit heuristics
  about 193-198
  committing, on characterization
    test complete 195, 196
  committing, on code in stable state 194
  committing, on feature completion 194
  committing, on preparatory
    refactoring completion 195
  committing, on unit test
    complete 196, 197
  committing, on written test
    for user scenario 194
commit types
  using 190-192
commit types, scenarios
  code, improving 191
  code, modifying 192
  defect, solving 191
  new feature 190
communication methods
  about 72, 73
  aggressive communication 73
  assertive communication 73
  right tone, using 74

right words, using 74
submissive communication 73

D

driver 24, 49
Driver-Navigator technique
  about 49
  advantages 49, 50
  disadvantages 50
  remarks 51
  rotation 49
  setup 49
  usage scenario 50
DSLR camera 119
dynamic microphones 179
dynamic range compression 180

E

editor functionalities 128
editor plugins, for remote
    pair programming
  about 132
  CodeTogether 132
  Floobits 133, 134
efficiency, boosting
  about 26
  breaks, taking 28, 29
  task switching, reducing 27, 28
elastic pair programming 161
elastic pairing
  about 62, 63
  advantages 63
  disadvantages 63, 64
  usage scenario 64
ensemble commits 162
ensemble programming 143

experiential learning 26
exploratory testing 17

F

facilitator 25, 26
Floobits
  about 133
  advantages 133
  disadvantages 133
frames per second (FPS) 116, 119, 175

G

Global Positioning System (GPS) 195
Google Meet
  about 139
  advantages 139
  disadvantages 139

H

headphones, for remote pair programming
  about 126
  in ear 126
  on ear 126
  over ear 126
heuristic 193
hypercardioid pattern 122

I

IDEs, for remote pair programming
  about 128
  CLion 131
  Intellij IDEA 129, 130

Tmux 132
Vim 131
Visual Studio Code 130, 131
incremental thinking 143
integrated development
    environment (IDE) 190
Intellij IDEA 129, 130

L

large-diaphragm condenser
    microphones 179
lateral thinking 34
Live Share 131
Live Share Audio 131

M

microphone
  Behringer C-1 123
  Electro-Voice RE20 123
  Rode Broadcaster 123
  selecting 122
  Shure SM7B 123
microphone, for external USB sound cards
  Behringer U-Phoria UMC22 124
  Behringer Xenyx 302USB 124
  Focusrite Scarlett Solo MKII 124
microphone, types
  dynamic microphones 179
  large-diaphragm condenser
      microphones 179
  small-diaphragm condenser
      microphones 179
mob.sh tool 144

N

navigator 25, 49

O

object-oriented programming
(OOP) language 156

P

Pairing-Trainee technique
about 51
advantages 52
disadvantages 52
remarks 53
rotation 52
setup 51
usage scenario 53
pair programming
about 41
anti-patterns 80, 81
audio, setting up 116
best practices 75-79
code review, feedback 14
collaborative work 7, 8
comfort, for future 15
complex domains, managing 13
complexities, managing in
complex domains 12
complexity, managing 6, 7
defect rate, minimizing 15
defining 24
difficult tasks 13
driver 24
exploratory testing 16
facilitator 25, 26
history 4, 5

Integrated Development Environment
(IDE), setting up 127
knowledge, advancing 9, 10
knowledge, leveling 8, 9
knowledge, sharpening 7
knowledge work 20
knowledge workers 20
navigator 25
new things, learning 41
organizing 68
problems, elucidating in pairs 5, 6
productivity, boosting 82
promiscuous pairing 69
round-robin pairing 68
scenarios 70, 71
selective pairing 70
social programming 42
staff liquidity 11, 12
system, improving 11
trainer 25, 26
video, setting up 116
wisdom, gaining 10
working 20
working solo, versus working in pair 72
pair programming setup
audio, checking 121, 122
cable connection, using 115
camera position 121
general technical requirements 174
internet connection, checking 114
lighting, checking 117, 118
microphone, positioning 125
mute pairing 126
portable router, using 115
two computers, using for coding 145
two computers, using for
remote screening 145
Wi-Fi connection, using 115

pair programming setup, camera selection
  about 119
  DSLR camera 119
  webcam 120
pair programming setup, headphones
  using 125, 126
pair programming setup,
      microphone selection
  about 122
  podcast microphone 123-125
pair programming setup, source control
  commit often 143
  ensemble commits 143, 144
  learning 141
  rotation 144
pair programming situations, limitations
  about 36
  lack of safe space 37, 38
  self pairing 38
  working alone 37
pair programming situations, usage
  about 29
  communication, improving 33, 34
  efficiency, increasing 30
  existing codebase, simplifying 35, 36
  knowledge transfer, aiding 31, 32
  problem-solving capabilities,
      enhancing 34, 35
  technical skills, improving 31
pair programming, source control
  rotation 144
pair programming style
  elastic pairing 62, 63
  improving 59
  strong-style pairing 64-66
  traditional pairing 60, 61
  unplanned pairing 59

pair programming techniques
  about 48
  Beginner-Advanced technique 53
  Beginner-Beginner technique 55
  Driver-Navigator technique 49
  Pairing-Trainee technique 51
  Ping-Pong technique 57
pair programming, with CEO
  about 17
  Rubber Duckling effect 19
  social programming 18
pair programming, with different
      specializations colleagues
  about 39
  pairing, with business analyst 41
  pairing, with tester 39, 40
  pairing, with UI designer 40
  pairing, with UI DevOps 40
personal security 207, 208
ping-pong 154
Ping-Pong technique
  about 57
  advantages 58
  disadvantages 58
  remarks 58
  rotation 57
  setup 57
  usage scenario 58
podcast microphone 123-125
Pomodoro technique 28, 29, 96-98
pop filter 180
Principle of Least Privilege 208
promiscuous pairing 69

Q

quality sound 175, 176
quality video 175, 176

R

random-access memory (RAM) 194
remote access, security
  about 207
  personal security 207, 208
  technical security 208, 209
remote access tools
  AnyDesk 204
  Chrome Remote Desktop 205
  evaluating 205
  Screen 204
  TeamViewer 203, 204
  working 202, 203
remote beginner-advanced technique
  about 156
  driver, remote specifics 157
  navigator, remote specifics 158, 159
  setup 157
remote driver-navigator technique
  about 150
  driver, remote specifics 151
  navigator, remote specifics 152, 154
  setup 150
remote elastic pair programming style
  about 161
  remote specifics 162, 163
  setup 162
remote pairing
  rules, recapping 202
remote pair programming
  anti-patterns 106, 107
  concerns 102-104
  distributed team 93, 94
  duration 95, 96
  good practices 104-106
  meeting 99
  organizing 88

purpose 89-92
  schedule 98, 99
  scope, deciding 95
  setting up 149, 150
  techniques and styles 148
remote pair programming,
    distributed team
  need for scenarios 94
remote pair programming, meeting
  business scope 100
  distributed team type, defining 100
  duration 100
  improvement ideas 101
  purpose, defining 100
  scheduling 100
  starting 101
  task types 100
  tools, deciding to use 101
  trainers and coaches, deciding 101
remote ping-pong technique
  about 154
  driver, remote specifics 155
  navigator, remote specifics 156
  setup 155
remote practices
  about 168
  remote breaks 168
  remote commit approach 169, 170
  secondary communication
    channel 168, 169
remote strong style
  about 163, 164
  remote specifics 165-167
  setup 165
retrospectives
  improving 110
  performing 107
  personal introspection 111

post actions 110
results, analyzing 110
schedule 107
techniques 108, 109
tools analysis 111
retrospectives, techniques
green 108
red 108
starfish 109
round-robin pairing 68
Rubber Duckling effect 19

S

safe refactoring 191
Screen
about 136, 204
advantages 136
disadvantages 136
screen sharing
AnyDesk 135
Google Meet 139, 140
Screen 136
settings 175
setting up 134
Skype 140, 141
TeamViewer 134, 135
Tuple 137
Use Together 137
Zoom 138
Secure Shell (SSH) 209
selective pairing 70
Single Sign-On (SSO) 138
Skype
about 140
advantages 140
disadvantages 140

small-diaphragm condenser
microphones 179
social programming 18, 42
social programming, disadvantages
about 43
bad coding practices 43
deployment time, learning 44
tension, within organization 44
tension, within team 43
unclear requirements 43
source control
using 188
source control rules
recapping 188
source control tools 141, 142
source control usage
improving 189, 190
speech enhancement
about 184
diction, employing 185
voice, warming up 185, 186
words, selecting 185
staff liquidity 11, 12
strong-style pairing
about 64-66
advantages 66
disadvantages 67
guideline, for communicating
to driver 65, 66
usage scenario 67
submissive communication 73
supercardioid pattern 122

T

Team Chat 131
TeamViewer
  about 134, 203, 204
  advantages 135
  disadvantages 135
technical debt 35
technical security 208, 209
Teddy Bear pair programming 19
Test-Driven Development (TDD) 57, 154
Tmux 132
tools
  relying on 206
traditional pairing
  about 60, 61, 159
  advantages 61
  disadvantages 61
  remote specifics 159-161
  setup 159
  usage scenario 62
trainer 25, 26
Tuple
  about 137, 138
  advantages 137
  disadvantages 138

U

unplanned pairing
  about 59
  advantages 60
  disadvantages 60
  usage scenario 60
USB external microphone
  about 124
  Behringer C-1U 124

Blue Yeti Studio Blackout 124
Rode NT-USB 124
Use Together
  about 137
  advantages 137
  disadvantages 137

V

video
  enhancing 176
  settings 175
  versus audio 174
video capture cards
  about 120
  Elgato Cam Link 120
  Epiphan AV.io HD or 4K 120
  Magewell USB Capture HDMI Plus 120
video conferencing tools
  about 117
  BlueJeans 117
  Google Hangout 117
  Google Meet 117
  Jitsi 117
  Skype 117
  Zoom 117
video enhancement
  camera 176, 177
  with green screen 177, 178
  with virtual background 178
Vim 131
Visual Studio Code 130, 131

W

webcam
  about 120
  Logitech C920e Pro 120

Logitech C922 Pro 120
Microsoft LifeCam HD-3000 120

Z

Zoom
  about 138
  advantages 138
  disadvantages 138

Printed in Great Britain
by Amazon

83812957R00140